How to Heal a Broken Heart

How to Heal a Broken Heart

From Rock Bottom to Reinvention*

*via ugly crying on the bathroom floor

ROSIE GREEN

First published in Great Britain in 2021 by Orion Spring
an imprint of The Orion Publishing Group Ltd
Carmelite House, 50 Victoria Embankment
London EC4Y 0DZ

An Hachette UK Company

1 3 5 7 9 10 8 6 4 2

The letters that appear in this book are composites of letters received by the
author. All names and identifying details have been changed or removed.

A CIP catalogue record for this book is
available from the British Library.

ISBN (Hardback) 978 1 3987 0129 8
ISBN (eBook) 978 1 3987 0131 1

Typeset by Born Group
Printed in Great Britain by Clays Ltd, Elcograf S.p.A

MIX
Paper from
responsible sources
FSC
www.fsc.org
FSC® C104740

www.orionbooks.co.uk

*To my beloved Aunt Liz, whose
innate goodness, endless generosity and capacity for
love will inspire me always*

CONTENTS

Implosion

It's 7.30 a.m. 2 Aug 2018. Our fifteenth wedding anniversary.

X's new work phone is charging. It sits on the kitchen work surface, its green light flashing malevolently.

I've never, ever looked at his phone without his knowledge, not once, but I've had an unfamiliar unease about a woman at his work in the last month so I type in X's code. It's the code he uses for everything and has done for all of the twenty-six years we've been together. It doesn't work. I feel a knot of dread. I go to my study and write until breakfast time.

'Can I look at your phone?' I ask X, over the granola. I see panic flash across his face.

'Why?'

'I'd like to see how a Galaxy phone works,' I say, with a faux nonchalance. 'What's the code?'

As he tells me and I type it in, I notice he is shaking.

I see he has WhatsApp. I didn't know he had WhatsApp. I click on it.

The kids argue about who gets the 'elephant' mug.

I click on to the messages.

I read them and feel stunned, sick, desperate.

The kids continue bickering. Time slows to a crawl. I feel like I'm viewing the situation from above, the picture of us flickering like an old home movie, disjointed, sepia. I run into the garden. X is frozen in the kitchen. I shout for him to follow me.

He does, finally.

I punch him in the chest. Hard.

Welcome to the Broken Hearts Club

This is how it all begins. The start of this story. And the end of life as I knew it.

I didn't see this coming. Didn't think my husband was unhappy. I didn't think that he would press destruct on our family life.

We met when we were eighteen years old. Were together by the time we were nineteen. Married for fifteen years. He was my constant. My safe port in any storm. Now I'm standing in our garden, my whole body shaking violently, my brain scrambling to make sense of it all, my eyes staring into his. This sudden stranger that I've known my entire adult life. At once I feel a stabbing pain, blindsided by the instant dissolution of years of security and safety. My mind races. I feel stupid, ashamed, angry. But mostly I feel hurt. And I'm terrified.

This day marks the start of a long, messy journey. There was no dramatic exit, Hollywood style, accompanied by a tear-jerking musical score and pyrotechnics. He didn't move out for months. Break ups are never as clean as we might imagine from the outside. Instead it was a slow, torturous exit that left my self-esteem trashed, my boundaries eroded, my physical self broken. By the time he finally left, I was a desperate woman, hardly able to eat or sleep. Prepared to sacrifice anything to keep my family together.

This may sound like a familiar story. It *is* a familiar story. It might be your story, too. But familiarity makes it no less cataclysmic when it happens to you.

Membership to the Broken Hearts' Club is one that no one wants. New members gain entry through desperation, dejection and soul-crushing sadness. Your welcome pack includes the horrible gut punch when you wake every morning. The grey cloud that sits over you day after day, meaning the kindness of others – flowers on your doorstep, sunlight, smiles – can't reach your soul.

Heartbreak happens every day but it doesn't happen to *you* every day. So when it does, it's a pain like no other. Which is why it's the stuff of tragedies, films and songs (all of which now speak directly to your heart). If you've just joined the club, I know right now you are in the blackest of holes. You've picked up this book because you need someone who understands. You need answers and, most of all, you need hope. Or your friend has bought it because you were howling on her kitchen floor yesterday and you scared the shit out of her (sorry, Em).

I hope by sharing my story, talking honestly about being dumped, rejected, left, abandoned and my subsequent road to recovery, I can help you see there is a path through the pain. One that, believe it or not (and I know you won't right now) will make you a stronger person, with more resilience and self-belief. I want to help you understand the brain's reaction to heartbreak and how, in an evolutionary misfire, we are wired to make things worse and hamper our own recovery (so you can blame your primate self for downing an entire bottle of white wine when you've only had Kettle Chips for dinner). I also want to show you that healing is a well-trodden path with some signposts that can help you move forward when you feel stuck. Though you think you will never feel better, will never want anyone else (and are convinced no one will ever want *you*) – I promise you can and will find happiness again.

When I was desperately scanning the shelves of my local bookshop for something, *anything* that would guide me through this steaming pile of shittiness, I couldn't find it. Lots of books were too academic and sterile, full of scientific advice that didn't seem to recognise the enormity of the maelstrom I was in. They were written by balding men who advised me to tap my chest and talked about heartbreak in an abstract way, as if it wasn't the thing that sliced your guts with cheese wire and consumed every waking thought. Then there were relationship coaches with wacky t-shirts and parrot earrings who suggested burning sage and cutting-cord rituals, neither of which I had to hand. Or twenty-somethings whose post-heartbreak rituals of vodka luges and polyamory bore no relation to my own life as a newly single mother of two with a full-time job and a school run.

In the meantime, I wrote about my break up for *Red* magazine, where for a decade I had written a light-hearted column about my happy family life. I felt sick at the idea of looking pathetic or sad, but writing was how I had always expressed what I was experiencing, good and bad. Seeing it in print – out there forever in public – was exposing and terrifying. But it was also cathartic, and the response was overwhelming.

The messages, cards and emails started arriving in their hundreds and then thousands. From women (and some men) who were in the throes of heartbreak or had been through it. People trapped in unhappy marriages, people who had experienced a family implosion in their childhood. Readers thanked me for my honesty, for not sugar-coating it or obscuring details to protect my ego. They identified with the feelings. They felt part of a community and that helped me to understand that, in my deep loneliness and pain, I was connected to thousands of others. They DM-d, emailed and wrote to say the article touched and connected with them like no other piece of writing.

A lot of my messages were from women whose husbands had left in a shocking fashion, who'd had affairs, then been angry, sometimes abusive and often cruel. Partners who had become unrecognisable from the person you thought they were. But I also heard from women who'd made the agonising decision to leave an unhappy marriage themselves. And people who had made a mutual decision to end a relationship that wasn't working but still struggled with the loneliness and uncertainty. Whatever kind of heartbreak you've gone through, whether you have behaved madly, badly or sadly (or, in likelihood, all three) you're welcome here. I hope you'll find solace, empathy, hope and some LOLs (yes, really).

In publishing this story I am braced for an accusation which is often levied at me: don't air your dirty linen in public. 'They' say you shouldn't talk about your husband's behaviour – whether cheating, falling out of love or just leaving – for the sake of your children. Or because that makes you sad and bitter and then no one will want you ever again. To which I give two fingers.

Elizabeth Day, author of *How to Fail*, believes in challenging 'the concept that there is a nobility in invisibility'. When I heard her say those words my already blossoming girl crush became borderline inappropriate. Because if we hide our feelings and gloss over the facts, then the splinter festers inside and you can never truly heal. Or learn. And we can't get a sense of perspective from our friends, or feel others' warmth, love, support

5

or advice. Instead our pain becomes a shameful and solitary secret.

This book is not about scoring points with my ex. There's no spite or desire for revenge; it's not a book full of stories that titillate with their awfulness (though Christ knows there were some). Because ultimately, that's unhelpful to my, and your, recovery. Your route from rock bottom to redemption is about YOU, not them.

Your situation might feel uniquely painful to you (and it is) but I promise you that you are on a path that many before you have trodden and you will find comfort and community in recognising this. We all go through stages of heartbreak from shock through to denial and bargaining to acceptance and hope (and many more). Recovery isn't linear and you might not progress through these stages methodically. You might slide down the snake from anger to depression or climb up a ladder from dating straight to happiness. But you will recognise so many of the emotions you are going through in all the chapters. So read this book however you like – skip forward and back and take from it what works for you.

My experience won't be a carbon copy of yours. But I hope by sharing it, it helps you heal, just like sharing it helped me.

CHAPTER ONE

Shock
(and ugly crying)

'I wish I could tell you it gets better, but it doesn't get better, you get better'
NICKY CLINCH

The pain of heartbreak is indescribable and yet to the outside world you bear no scars. You are entirely broken but look the same as you did the day before your world blew apart. It is almost inconceivable that others can't see your misery because it feels physical. It's in your head but it consumes every cell of your body.

Each of us experiences the pain in different ways but for me, at its most manageable, heartbreak feels like a dull, background ache that you can't shake off. A deep, damp sorrow. A constant unease gnawing at the soul. Then sometimes, out of nowhere, or out of somewhere, it ramps up to unbearable levels of intensity.

So powerful that your body involuntarily expels it in guttural howls or sobs. So all-consuming it makes you pull at your hair and pace the room. Press your nails into your skin and watch as the blood bubbles to the surface.

Words inflict this pain. Not sticks and stones.

My heartbreak feels more debilitating, more soul destroying than any other emotion I have ever experienced. Other sadnesses that should logically and morally sit above it, involving my children or lost lives, don't compare. I'm slightly ashamed to admit this, but it's the truth: heartbreak hurts more than anything.

A friend of mine, whose husband died suddenly at the same time my relationship fell apart, told me, 'I think it's worse for you. At least I knew M loved me.' I appreciated her honesty.

Because I have to confess to some darker moments in which I wished my own husband had died rather than left me. It felt (forgive me) less humiliating. In my imagined alternative universe as a widow, I saw myself dressed up like Jackie O at the funeral in a veil and Dolce dress, nodding to mourners in a dignified manner. And cashing in the life insurance . . .

My Google history betrays my tortured state of mind in those early days of devastation. It feels like a cassette tape, pulled out, scrambled and scratched. It's full of 4 a.m. searches for anything that will validate my pain or give me hope that things can be repaired. Questions I put to Google: can you die from a broken heart? How do you make your husband fall back in love with you?

Impact of marital separation on children? How long to get over a divorce? Do women and children get to stay in the family home post-divorce? How much is a boob job? Is [insert childhood crush, university flirtation, workplace fixation] married?

I read voraciously about celebrity infidelity and rejection – there's something reassuring about the fact this shit can happen to women with multimillion-dollar pay cheques and a thigh gap. In case you feel the same, here are some gorgeous, successful and award-winning women who have been heartbroken. Publicly . . .

Jennifer Garner
Sienna Miller
Beyoncé
Nicole Kidman
Reese Witherspoon
Sandra Bullock
Cher
Elizabeth Hurley
Hillary Clinton
Uma Thurman
Elle Woods (OK, she's not real)
Liberty Ross

I returned to this list time and again, like a soothing talisman. Would you suggest that Reese Witherspoon or Beyoncé (Beyoncé!) were somehow to blame for their own heartbreak? Would you diss the magnificence that is Cher and find her somehow lacking in a way that would make a man look elsewhere? Do you think that if only Sienna

Miller had been prettier she'd have kept her man's eyes
on her, not the nanny? But I bet in the long, desperately
dark nights you sometimes blame yourself, don't you? I
know because I did. If that's you, take my talisman list
(or make your own) and use it to remind yourself that
this crap happens to everyone. And we get over it, too.

In my incessant googling about heartbreak, I came
across American psychologist Guy Winch and his TED
talk, called 'How to Fix a Broken Heart'. I watched it
on repeat and sometimes I still do. There's something
about his scientific approach to heartbreak that comforts
me. It makes me feel less alone, more like I'm going
to survive. His reassuring talk suggests the grief is a
process and that it's normal to feel like your world has
ended. It might help you, too.

Guy talks about just how off-the-scale shit heartbreak
feels. Only he doesn't use those exact words. He says
'romantic rejection', AKA being dumped, abandoned,
ghosted or just told 'I'll leave it there', properly hurts.
Physically. He points to an experiment done by Ethan
Kross at Michigan University which compared sharp
emotional pain and sharp physical pain. Volunteers who
had been through a recent devastating break up were
placed in an MRI scanner and shown a picture of their ex.
Their brain response was measured. Then they repeated
the experiment but this time the volunteers were exposed
to pain via a hot probe on their arm, the heat cranked
up to a level described as 'almost unbearable'. When
the scientists compared the results of the MRI scans,

they found that exactly the same areas of the brain were activated by the emotional pain as by the physical pain.

So just because heartbreak is invisible, doesn't mean it doesn't hurt. Actual science says it's almost unbearable. I found this a comforting thought when I was tempted to beat myself up for my reactions in those early days.

IT'S PHYSICAL

I couldn't eat. I couldn't sleep. I couldn't focus. My heart raced and my body shook.

Does yours?

Turns out that's 'normal' too.

I researched the physiological effects of heartbreak for a piece I was writing and discovered that, in a break up, the feel-good hormones dopamine and oxytocin crash out of your body, replaced by the much less pleasant cortisol and adrenalin. Cortisol and adrenalin can affect your coping mechanisms, causing a racing heart, diarrhoea and nausea. And as if that's not enough, they also compromise your immune system.

Heartbreak can trigger muscle weakness, exhaustion and insomnia. And sometimes make you feel like you are going to die. I learnt about this when a friend of mine took herself to A&E, convinced she was having a heart attack. The doctors told her she had broken heart syndrome. It shares many of the same symptoms as a heart attack, like changes in heart rhythm and blood substances. In extreme cases it can cause a weakening of the heart muscle, which can be fatal when the heart can't pump enough blood to meet the body's needs. (So don't let anyone tell you you're being melodramatic when you say, 'I feel like I'm dying.')

Broken heart syndrome also goes by the name Takotsubo syndrome. Takotsubo is Japanese for 'octopus pot' and the syndrome is named because the emotional devastation of a bad break up can stun the heart, causing the left ventricle to change shape like the narrow neck of an octopus trap.

So you are entitled to feel bad. This shit is serious.

'Heartbreak is a trauma,' says Nicky Clinch, spiritual mentor, maturation coach and one of my go-to women for unravelling emotions. I first came across her when I interviewed her for a magazine piece years ago and was struck by her mixture of empathy, sage advice and zero BS. When heartbreak hit, she was one of the experts I looked to for advice.

Trauma, *noun*:
1. A deeply distressing or disturbing experience.
2. A physical injury.

'Trauma puts us into a state of shock,' says Nicky. 'It's a form of protection emotionally and physically, stopping us feeling all the pain at once.' She says it is common for those experiencing heartbreak to 'numb out and disassociate. To feel like you are leaving the body.'

I experienced this. To me, numbing out meant that I sometimes felt detached as my kids howled with raw emotional pain. Or when friends' eyes filled with tears as I told them that X was leaving. It often felt like it was happening to someone else. It was as if I couldn't absorb their pain as well, so my brain deflected it. Like Teflon. Previously, if my children had been snubbed by a school friend or dropped from their sports team I would have felt the anguish with them, but not now. Now I could only cope with my own grief.

Heartbreak precipitates a tsunami of emotions, many of which are hard for your brain to deal with and may manifest as physical symptoms. As well as disassociation and emotional numbness, the effects of shock and trauma associated with heartbreak can include hyper-ventilating, feeling crazily overtired and panic attacks.

I feel lucky to have avoided panic attacks as, Nicky says, these are very common in the first throes of a break up because the mind is trying to control something you can't control.

What are panic attacks? The NHS describes them as a rush of intense mental and physical symptoms, which can come on very quickly and for no apparent reason. They can include a racing heartbeat, feeling faint, sweating, nausea, chest pain, shortness of breath, trembling, hot flushes, chills, shaky limbs, a choking sensation, dizziness, numbness or pins and needles, dry mouth and feeling like you're not connected to your body. You might describe them as horrifically, off-the-scale frightening.

13

What can you do to alleviate the symptoms of a panic attack? At school, someone would always appear with a paper bag and tell you to breathe into it. I remember in fourth year someone gave Karen V a plastic bag, rather than paper, which seemed like a sure-fire route to asphyxiation to me. These days the advice is to breathe slowly and deeply, not to fight the sensations and to focus on peaceful relaxing images. If you suffer from panic attacks regularly, longer term you might be prescribed talking therapies or anti-depressants.

The human brain struggles with uncertainty at any time and feeling completely out of control at this stage of a relationship break up is common and can have a huge impact.

Are you in control?

I was not. My carefully crafted life was collapsing. In an attempt to create the security I had wanted so desperately as a kid, at eighteen years old I went for the strongest, steadiest, most moral man I could find. A man who loved me a little bit more than I loved him. I thought that would keep us safe.

It didn't work.

Like a car skidding on ice, I spent those early months of the break up desperately trying to steer us back on course, even though all along my body was braced for the impact that I knew was coming. I spent months with a clenched jaw, in a constant state of fight or flight, waking everyday with dread squatting in my mind.

I hate, hate, hate feeling out of control. Perhaps you do too? Perhaps you're trying to regain control by forcing your partner to come home? By begging them to reconsider? By threatening them with what they will lose?

Our difficulty in dealing with uncertainty is partly why a break up makes you feel so abjectly terrible because if this certainty ends then what unknown future is coming? Yes, you might miss the past or present – the way his brow furrows when he concentrates or the warmth of his hugs – but part of the desperation you feel about losing someone is loss of the future you imagined. The future you both signed up to. A break up means everything that was certain, now isn't. Everything you knew to be true, you now question.

I tried to get us back on track by sheer force of will. 'You do love me,' I'd tell him firmly. 'You don't want to leave me.' He would seem to nod and agree, but then, after a bottle of wine or a night out it would change again. I felt at my worst when I was trying to convince myself we both wanted to save our marriage, when, really, he was done.

An aside: sometimes my mind goes back to when X asked me to marry him. When he seemed so totally in love. When he was shaking with nerves. Now I think, did he mean it when he proposed or was he just following the crowd, doing what everyone else was doing? In our frequent and fraught conversations about the future, I felt like he referred to our whole marriage as if was some kind of mistake. Did he never really love me? In my heart I know this is not true, but still it messes with my head.

When you are in the pits of hell, facing into the abyss of loneliness and emptiness that is separation, it can be tempting to hold on to your relationship at all costs. But you know as well as I do, waiting for the plaster to be ripped off is worse than just doing it. At least when you do hit rock bottom, when all hope is extinguished, the only way is up. I can't tell you when that moment will come for you but I can tell you from experience that your lowest point is also your turning point.

Hypnotherapist, NLP practitioner and master coach Malminder Gill says that we feel more anxiety over uncertainty than we do about negative experiences when they actually happen. Our brain knows how to cope when it is certain of a bad situation – when the outcome is bad but also clear. But the brain struggles to cope when we anticipate things that haven't yet happened or create uncertainties or potential threats.

That's why we often end up finishing relationships even when we don't want to. They are limping along, bleeding out, and we know it's more humane to ourselves to kill it dead. Often the person who wants out is not brave enough to call time on the relationship and so they just act in a horrific way until the other person has to do it themselves.

You carry round that hideous sinking feeling, the same one you do when you know they want you out of your job at work. I knew our fatally injured relationship was all wrong, I knew I should end it and tell X in no uncertain terms to shove his disrespectful treatment of me, but I couldn't bear to. In fact, it was the last thing I wanted.

Did you have to finally call time on your relationship because they couldn't bear to be the bad guy?

Friends and readers of my columns and articles have told me they had to be the ones to utter the words 'it's over' even though their exes had obviously checked out a long time ago. Often, not always, boomeranging into the arms of another. Another generalisation? Women tend to be braver about pulling the plug. In fact, Greg Behrendt alludes to this his book *He's Just not That into You* when he says of men that they would 'rather lose an arm out of a city bus window than tell you simply, "You're not the one."'

When your world is imploding it helps to create certainties. I told myself some simple ones. My friends and family will always be here for me. I will always have a roof over my head. I have the love of my children. That this will pass.

What are your certainties? Yours may be different to mine but there will be something solid to hold on to. Find it and remind yourself of it as often as you need.

Even if it's only, 'there will always be wine'. Or taxes.

The former is a more pleasant thought.

I remember that my phone became the harbinger of uncertainty. The portal through which, by absentia, X showed me he had checked out. For months I lived and died by the ping. Waited for it. Decoded it. Showed it to friends. Sometimes I would leave home for a run, or for tea/wine with friends, without my phone as if I didn't care, while praying for his notification when I got home. A notification that would magically communicate that it was all OK. That he wanted back in. That he was committed to making it work. That he loved me and it had all been a huge mistake.

It never was.

In the end, I found the only way I could get control was to turn off my phone. If you're not strong enough, get someone else to do it for you, or to keep your phone away from you when you're feeling vulnerable.

REJECTION MAKES YOU CRAZY
(SCIENCE SAYS SO)

If uncertainty feels shit, rejection is worse, right?

As humans we are repulsed by rejection, conditioned to find it deeply unpalatable. We are always given the tools to explain it away. You didn't get the part? The casting director must have been shagging that other girl. She didn't pick you to be her bridesmaid? It's because she knew you hated coral and satin. You didn't make a second interview? They don't know what they are doing. He didn't ask you on a second date? It must be because you intimidated him.

At the core of my break up pain was rejection. At first, my brain would short-circuit to any emotion to get away from facing the rejection – I'd rather feel sadness, anger, fear, anything. But a part of me recognised that the onion of layers of sorrow, anger and disbelief are just wrapped around a solid core of rejection. He didn't want me. And that hurts the most. It was rejection that made me sob in the shower, turning up the pressure so the kids couldn't hear my desperate gasps. Rejection that caused my tears to fall when talking to my friends, leaving muddy mascara streaks on the phone screen.

According to psychologist and author of *Mirror Thinking: How Role Models Make Us Human,* Fiona Murden, rejection feels so bad because it dramatically affects how we see ourselves. She explains, 'Rejection undermines our personal narrative. Which means it goes to the very core of who we believe ourselves to be. The story we tell ourselves about ourself. It calls into question our whole identity.'

This combination of rejection and uncertainty make for a headfuck like no other. If I am not X's beloved wife, who lives in a country idyll with two beautiful children, I thought, then who am I? A single mother whose husband has decided he'll pass, if that's OK? The

19

fact I'd written about my husband and our perfectly imperfect life for hundreds of thousands of people made it all the more humiliating. I had to let go of this identity and assume a new one. Spurned wife? Has a great ring, no?

One of the worst things about a break up is that it makes you feel like you are going bat-shit crazy, that you have lost control of your rational self. And you are not wrong. So intense is the situation that your subconscious mind kicks in and makes you do all kind of weird shit like, ahem, stand and wait at a station for an hour in the middle of the night for someone who'd rather see anyone but you when they get off the train.[1]

Or spend hours trying to bypass their EE security to see who they are calling.[2]

In the early stage of a break up, your brain seems to actively sabotage your recovery. It's as if your own thinking, which is supposed to be on your side, is actively trying to mess you up. Anthropologist Helen Fisher, whose TED talks on love get millions of views, says that the irony of being dumped is that you want to forget the person but the rejection makes you love them harder than ever. I know this to be 100 per cent true. In the throes of rejection, I wanted X more than I ever had before.

Helen says that the intense emotion of rejection makes you willing to risk anything to get them back. Anything.

---

1 Me

2 Me again

Her research demonstrates the science behind this intensity and obsession. When recently rejected people were shown pictures of their exes, the brain showed activity in the reward/motivation areas. This activity releases dopamine. Dopamine is a bit like Pringles – you always want more. So, in an evolutionary fuck up, these obsessive thoughts are triggered whether you are falling hard for someone or obsessing over an ex. Hence you spend all day chasing the dopamine hit by thinking about the person who has just shat on you. Dopamine bypasses the conscious part of our brain so we literally lose control, doing more and more desperate things to get satisfaction. This is why you stalk their Instagram (a lot), call their mates to chat it through (AKA gain intel), talk about them ad nauseam and quite possibly sit outside their work (OK, just me then . . .). The more you look the more you want to look.

I found it really helpful to understand that my brain was making me behave in this way because a) it made me feel less like a loser, b) I felt like if I understood it I could get a handle on it and c) when I called friends at 6 a.m. to decode text messages, I could tell them my subconscious brain made me do it.

And, like the obsessive thinking isn't enough, it turns out that heartbreak makes your brain crave your ex like an addict does smack.

I went to bed thinking about my ex. Woke up thinking about him. Craved his reassurances desperately and insatiably. Which is weird because previous to this I

21

had been pretty well adjusted on that front. Not needy. Not jealous. I didn't recognise my own behaviour. I was never the girl who needed hourly calls. Who tracked phones. Or steamed open envelopes.

When I said to my friend J that I felt X had been body snatched, she replied that she thought the same of me; the feisty, take-no-shit Green had been replaced by a woman she didn't recognise. Someone so desperate to keep her family together she'd sacrifice her dignity.

In the book that accompanies his TED talk on heartbreak (in the early days these books were arriving at my door with more regularity than the baked goods my lovely friends were trying to tempt me to eat), Guy Winch says that romantic love shares the same neurochemistry that is associated with addiction. And that means that when the drug, or the person we love, is taken away, we go through actual withdrawal. That results in cravings, inability to focus, sleep disturbance, appetite issues, crying, depression and intense feelings of loneliness that can only be cured by our drug/person. Sound familiar?

That was exactly how I felt. Compelled to pick the scab. Mortifyingly undignified in my need to be reassured. And then there is the why, why, why?

If your mate starts hanging out with someone else you can shrug it off and think they just need to be with someone different right now. If you didn't get the job you can go out, inhale some salted nuts, drink your body weight in rosé and chalk it up to wrong time, wrong personality combo. But when you get dumped it feels impossible to be rational.

Why are we so obsessed with the why?

Because your entire identity is at stake here. You are desperately trying to find an answer that feels palatable.

Fiona Murden talks me through how our brain works: 'The prefrontal cortex has evolved in humans to enable us to plan, analyse, sort, and explain things in our environment. We're able to remove or change the things that we don't like – for our ancestors that may have meant running away from a predator; for us it may mean moving out of an area we don't like living in, or changing jobs if we don't like our boss, or if we don't like an item of clothing, returning it. We then believe we can use this strategy on our own thinking, turning this in on our mind to make sense of our emotions and to try and control them. In fact, we are brought up to believe that's what we should do, e.g. "come on, don't cry" or "you really shouldn't be thinking about that". But when we're under a lot of pressure, or stressed, trying to control our thoughts and emotions just doesn't work.

'Firstly, our prefrontal cortex can't hold that much information at once so it can very quickly become overwhelmed. Secondly, when we are feeling emotional the emotional centres of our brain tend to be in the driving seat. Those bits of the brain are far from rational so analysis simply doesn't work. Added to which there's the push and pull between the rational saying what we "should" be feeling and the emotional saying what we *are* feeling, whether we like it or not. So we end up tying ourselves up in knots and getting increasingly stressed because we can't do what we're trying to (i.e. work out what we're feeling and why, or what happened and why). The more we try to analyse our emotions the more complex they become. It's a bit like when you can't get to sleep – the harder you try, the more difficult it becomes; the more you worry about it, the more awake or anxious you seem to get.'

Sometimes, when searching for the why, my brain lets me give up and create my own story. A story that neatly absolves him of responsibility and allows me to believe he still loves me and respects me. This way my dream of happy ever after can stay intact.

Only it isn't true and I know it. Which really, really hurts.

There's a theory that the hamster-wheel thoughts are because your brain is at DEFCON one. Full alert. It's taking this very seriously. Why does rejection take such premier position in your brain? Some scientists believe it's because heartbreak is an evolutionary issue. For early female humans, the bond between you and a mate is a pretty important factor in whether you (and, if you have them, your offspring) are going to stay alive. So you are hardwired to focus on it. Hence the never-ending wonderings about where they are, who they are with and how the fuck can they think life is going to be better without you and your signature chicken dish?

24

Some of my heartbroken mates report being stuck with a constant reel of Hallmark moments ticker taping through their brain. Like those sodding 'memories' moments that your phone flashes up (the person who thought up these should be forced to watch *Keeping Up with the Kardashians* on repeat for the rest of their life as penance). Guy Winch's theory is that it's the same as when a child burns itself on a hot stove and the searing pain reminds them not to do it again. Only in this scenario, the brain wants to make heartbreak so horrendous you don't do it again. And by throwing up all the good stuff, it dials up the agony to its most unbearable.

I felt overwhelmed by the future without him. Without an 'us'. My brain fast forwarded to telling the kids, breaking up the house, the fact my pension pot is more like a sodding thimble. To what happens when the smoke alarm goes off at 3 a.m.? Or if there is a burglar? Or how I'm going to do whatever he does to the boiler to make it work?

X said he loved me, but not in that way any more. He wouldn't kiss me on the lips. He didn't want to sleep in our bed. He seemed to have zero empathy for my pain. Only irritation. He stayed out for nights on end and those nights were the worst of my life. So long, so dark. I tried controlled breathing to sleep but that's about as effective as a Dettol colonic is on Covid. I took sleeping pills to stop the incessant chatter in my head. Sometimes I clawed at the bedsheets in sheer desperation, crying in my sleep. I woke at one, three, five – my face tight with dried tears. Nights were full of vivid dreams. I'd sleepwalk through the days.

The only thing that eased my pain was talking to friends and family. I chain smoked through calls to them. Looking to each of them to fill this void, to talk me down from the ledge. Through my shroud of grey I could just, only just, feel the warmth of their love and their concern. Jen, my BF since Brownies, slept in my bed one particularly bad night. Tania spent hundreds of pounds calling from Abu Dhabi.

They always picked up when I called.

At my lowest, I heard about Sara Davison, a divorce coach. I drove to her house in Ascot, and told her my tale, in between sobs. She listened and dispensed some practical advice on how to deal with getting through each day. It changed a lot for me. I wished I had heard it sooner and so now I want to share it with you.

Sara's advice:

1. Create a mental stop sign and pull it out when you are about to go down that rabbit hole of stalking.
2. Exercise. Why? Because it's hard to focus on murderous/agonising thoughts when your lungs feel like the GB weightlifting team is sitting on your chest.
3. Distract yourself with whatever works. For me this is listening to *The Archers* (did I just admit that publicly?), reading *Hello* magazine, watching a rom com or sharing a bottle of medicinal rosé with mates.

4. Stop romanticising. Take off the rose-tinted glasses –
   which your brain really wants you to keep on, BTW
   – and list all the things you really don't like about
   your ex. The way they shovelled in their food like
   a half-starved boar at a trough or left their toenail
   clippings on the side of the bath.
5. Avoid avoidance tactics. Partying, over exercising,
   working 24/7, drinking won't help with recovery. 'In
   fact lack of sleep, or using alcohol and drugs, can lead
   to depression and actually enhance negative feelings.'
   *N.B. I learnt (the hard way) that going out and drinking my
   bodyweight was a one-way ticket to paranoiaville the next day.*
6. And don't shag the gardener/school dad who has
   always had the hots for you, however tempting.

When a potential number six appeared on my horizon,
Nicky urged me not to use a rebound relationship as a
band-aid. 'The greatest way to block out any pain is to
fall in love with someone else,' she said. 'Love is one
of the biggest drugs there is – as is sex – but it always
comes to bite you on the bottom if you go straight
into a relationship without working on yourself first. It
never works and it never lasts.'

I didn't want to 'work on myself'. Those three
words always made me want to slam my head on the
table whenever they were trotted out by celebrities in
the glossy magazine interviews I did for my day job.
And I really didn't want to 'face my emotions', as
Sara Davison suggested. In fact, I'd rather have licked

27

Donald Trump's armpits. But she explained that the best way to get clarity on your negative emotions is to confront head on how they make you feel. Make space and time to feel sad, or angry, or scared. 'It will take away the fear and de-intensify their power over you.'

Her other suggestion was gratitude. Which again made me think WTAF? Grateful you've been done over? Be grateful your heart is smashed into a thousand pieces? Grateful that your husband has fucked off and couldn't give a shit?

But gratitude really does make you feel better. Research by Dr Robert A. Emmons has shown it decreases toxic emotions like envy, regret and frustration and increases happiness and self-esteem. All of which seems sensible. And rational.

But sometimes I could be neither and I was just floored. Floored by this stranger I'd known for decades. Floored that he could be so cold in the face of my distress.

X arrived back from three nights sleeping at the office and I met him at the station. He was irritated by this. He looked at me so coldly. I couldn't believe this was the same man who had always looked at me the way Harry does Meghan. The man that seemed so utterly devoted to me, his kids and his life.

I stared at the ground, muted with pain. He seemed angry with me for crying. How could he be so detached? He 'may not love me in that way' any more, but didn't he care at all? Suddenly I irritated him. Repulsed him. My brain couldn't process it.

28

'I just don't feel the same way.'

When I asked him to expand on this (maybe not in those words) he just said that he loves me as a friend. He doesn't want to live with me. Doesn't want to 'be' with me.

And this is the headfuck. Of often not ever knowing why they choose to leave. The truth feels vital to making sense of it. Do they not fancy you any more? Do they fancy someone else? Or are they, as they are saying, just not in love with you any more.

So many women write and email me. They say 'my husband has suddenly changed. He says he wants out of our marriage or he doesn't love me any more.' And I want to say, 'He is probably having an affair.' Because the truth is, 90 per cent of the time, that's what's happening. He may have already wanted out, he may have been unhappy, but an affair is often the catalyst for leaving, it gives many men the strength to be so brutal, the push they need to walk out of the door. They might say it changes nothing, but it changes everything. If your brain is scrambling to make sense of their behaviour and you don't know every piece of the jigsaw, it can tip you further into hell.

Psychologist Fiona Murden says, 'If someone is cheating, they are not going to tell you that. And when they deny it, you believe what they are saying, because they are the person in the world closest to you. And that's what makes it so difficult and traumatic. The disconnect between what is happening and what

29

you are being told eats away at your self-esteem and self-belief. Causes you to question your sanity.'

I still think it's one of the cruellest things you can do to someone. To not fess up. To tell them instead you just 'don't feel that way about them any more'. Because while that in itself might be true, when there is someone else in the wings it changes everything. The cheater has changed direction, changed allegiances, has a body pumped full of lust and longing. They are craving their fix of the other person. And their partner's neediness and questioning are an obstacle to this. A downer on their excitement.

Our break up was not straightforward, which made things worse. There were reconciliations. There was counselling. X told me, more than once, he was not leaving for anyone else. He said this to the counsellor. Some things made this believable. Some things didn't.

I was a mess. I sobbed so much on the bus once that a stranger came up to me and handed me a pack of tissues, her face full of kindness and empathy.

Some days I didn't want to go on.

My cousin forwarded me an email from a colleague. She'd read my piece in *Red* and wanted to tell me her story. I found comfort in her words because they made me feel less like I had done something terrible to bring this all about and more like this might be more about his shit than mine. It gave me hope when I felt none. And it made me think about all the other people in my position who were not lucky enough to get the letters and the DMs and the cards that I did, reminding me I was not alone in this.

So here it is. I hope it helps.

Hi Rosie

I have just read your article and can completely identify with it. My husband walked out on me three years ago after fifteen years of marriage, saying he no longer loved me. It came as a terrible shock and left me completely devastated. He was in fact having an affair with a much younger woman – his personal trainer from the high-end fitness club he'd joined – which he totally denied until a friend of mine caught him red handed and he had to admit she'd been on the scene since the start of our troubles.

He's a typical alpha male / narcissist – very charming and good-looking, life and soul of the party, etc. I went through all the same heartbreak as you've been through – unable to eat, barely able to function at work, carrying that awful heavy feeling around in my heart all the time, experiencing a total apathy with life, turning to anti-anxiety medication to help take the edge off the pain . . . He then proceeded to bounce back in and out of my life for two years – each time I was pulling myself together he'd pop back up, full of apologies, sweeping me off my feet, showering me in gifts, saying he'd made a massive mistake and loved me, etc. etc. Stupidly I'd fall for it every time, even after he'd had a stint living with the PT and then throwing her out. I just wanted my old life back I guess and he was so persuasive, plus I did genuinely love him despite his faults.

31

Anyway after the seventh time of taking him back, I got all the indicators one weekend that he was about to up and go again so when he went out to get us coffees on Sunday morning, I literally packed up all his bags for him and threw him out, blocked him from my phone and have not seen or spoken to him since. Luckily, I'd already divorced him over the two years of yo-yoing so had been through that ultimate sadness.

Now, fifteen months on, I've got my life back on track, have a fabulous set of friends who supported me through all the awfulness and am in a new relationship with a lovely man. Life is very different to what it was pre the devastation my ex wreaked on it but I'm getting to the stage where actually I think he's done me a favour and it may well be better in the long run. It was a terrible journey which I would not wish on my worst enemy but in time it does get better, no matter how awful it feels at the time, and I firmly believe everything happens for a reason – we just don't always recognise it at the time.

Cxx

Something in us keeps us going. It does. Even if you feel like you can't bear it. Take it from me. Take it from others who have been here before you.

Mylene Klass, when she had her heart spliced by her first husband, said, 'I just had to keep going because my girls would be up every morning and asking me to make breakfast or fetch their recorders. My girls saved me.'

The 'recorders' got me. Your world has stopped but

assemblies/nit checks/World sodding Book Day waits for no woman.

But even if it's not children that get you up, a life force will. It's a period of intensity. Of all the feels. When songs speak directly to you. I remember walking past a tube poster. It said: 'Your value does not decrease based on someone's inability to see your worth.'

Hold on to this. It helps.

HEARTWORK

Books to read:

I Can Mend Your Broken Heart by Hugh Willbourn and Paul McKenna

This is the kind of promise I need. This book explains a lot about the psychology of a split and has some useful ways to reframe the experience. It gives you exercises to work through, which help, even if some of the exercises (tapping) feel a bit left field for me.

How to Fix a Broken Heart by Guy Winch

Winch is a psychologist who has helped counsel the dejected and rejected for decades. His book looks at why the brain behaves the way it does and in doing so helps us get clarity on the head-fuckery that is heartbreak. Also seek out his brilliant TED talk.

Five things people said that made me feel better

7. I'm here for you.
8. Call me anytime.
9. You will be OK.
10. Can I have the kids for a while?
11. This rosé is medicinal.

Five things people said that made me feel worse

1. I'm going to be extra nice to my husband now.
2. Did you give him enough blow jobs?
3. Are you going to have to sell the house?
4. Is there someone else involved?
5. You'll have to get naked in front of someone new.

CHAPTER TWO

Denial
(mind fuckery)

'He must have a frontal lobe tumour'

You've got that pit-of-stomach feeling upon waking. A gnawing doubt that is eating away at your soul. You can't focus on anything except them. Your head is spinning with so many untruths. So many unpalatable new truths.

This has to be the shittiest stage. When it comes to rock bottom, this is it. When the flame of hope isn't yet extinguished. You are desperately fanning the embers, hoping for a miracle. But it feels like there is only one of you still in this. The truth has somehow become subjective. Your truth versus their truth. Distorted by the intensity with which you, and they, need to believe the stories you are telling yourselves. Suddenly you are questioning everything. The secure, stable foundations underpinning your life have crumbled to dust and yet denial abounds.

Whatever your break up story, and there are so many different ones out there, some things are always the same. There will be gut-twisting doubts, endless questions, a fear of the future and the abject misery of knowing the person you love is now free to find another. They might be sleeping in a new bed, quite possibly with someone else. Living a new life in which you are the side show, rather than the main event. And when the person you trust implicitly, the person you have shared everything with, the person who is the emergency contact number in your passport, the person who watched you walk down the aisle and held your hand as your babies were being delivered, refuses to be straight with you, it fractures everything you believe in, right?

This headfuck is exponentially increased if the person in question was previously of 'good moral character', a person who prides themselves on a righteous code so strong you believe it runs through them like letters through seaside rock. A person who wouldn't even let the kids eat a packet of crisps as they walked round the supermarket and pay for the empty packet at the till. A person who has always insisted on walking on the outside of the pavement, like the chivalrous hero out of an Austen novel, lest a carriage come past and spray you with mud.

When that person feels gone forever, it's hard to de-cipher how much of what you are thinking is paranoia and how much simply rational conclusion. Every break up stirs up the silt, makes things murky, clouds reason, distorts memories. We replay events over and over in our minds – trying to understand what happened, our role in it, what they are thinking and what the 'truth' is. I'm sure your brain is, like mine was, scrambled.

Here is a story that played over and over in my mind in the denial phase of my break up:

A week or so later he needs to work late and to stay at the office overnight. I feel sick at the prospect but the power balance in our relationship has tipped so completely in his favour I no longer feel I can risk voicing my angst.

He says I have to trust him or it won't work. I know somewhere deep down this is wrong. How can you trust someone so quickly after they took a sledgehammer and smashed up your self-esteem? But I don't say so because I can't risk it all crashing down.

That night I can't sleep. Every time I tap my phone to see the time, only another few minutes have crawled past. Its torture. I'm wracked with anxiety, consumed with fear. I want to reach out for reassurance but I know it will irritate him.

At 6 a.m. I try to call him. His phone is off. He had said he would leave it on.

I remembered hearing about a friend who had tracked their husband's phone.

I go downstairs. As I activate the search I hold my breath. I'm shaking. I have never, ever done anything like this before. The arrow drops down with offensive ease and clarity. It seems to indicate that his phone is not at his office but instead way across London, near what looks to be a budget hotel.

At 7 a.m. he answers. He says he is at his office and not miles away in the SE suburbs.

I try desperately to believe him. I search Google for justifications. Maybe his phone ran out of battery there late last night, so that is where it recorded its last signal? I check again but it is still saying he is in south-east London.

I finally get through to him again. I feel so deranged I ask X to take pictures of his office. He sends through pictures that to me could or could not be his office. His face is grey and grim.

I say that I am sorry.

Phones can tell untruths. But so can people.

I wished I could channel Eva Longoria, who said of her split with Tony Parker, 'It wasn't about who he chose. I had moments of like: "OK, I'm not sexy enough? I'm not pretty enough? Am I not smart enough?" Then I immediately stopped. "No, no, no – don't start doing that." Because you can get stuck in that cycle and you can carry that on to other things.'

I craved Eva's certainty. Her self-respect. She knew – she believed – he was the one with the problem, not her. I wanted to be that strong, but I wasn't. I was a ball of paranoia and doubt. If you are like me, at this stage your anxiety has reached nuclear proportions. You want to tear at your skin, pull at your hair and claw at your face.

'Could he lie?' I asked my friends, incessantly. 'Could he?'

At the height of my paranoia I remembered that, a year previously, I had interviewed psychologist Andrew Marshall for a piece on the 'manopause'. This turned out to be eerily prescient. But more on that later. Somehow I felt Andrew might have the answer to my lying question, so I emailed him. At 2 a.m.

How can people lie to their partners?

He responded gratifyingly early because he was in Germany and, well, time difference.

'Affairs happens in a parallel world, a side world where it has no impact,' he wrote. 'They (the person having the affair) put it in a box over there. They are so much in crisis they don't think it through. They will minimise the problems. They will say to themselves, "It doesn't matter about the hurt I am causing, because we love each other." If you have an affair you need to have watertight boxes. To shut down your thinking.'

So yes, 'good' people can lie. They are probably even lying to themselves in order to continue the deception, the illusion that they are doing nothing wrong. They might tell themselves, 'I deserve this', that their partner did something that 'made them cheat', that they 'didn't have a choice'.

When someone you thought you knew so well acts far out of character, it is destabilising in the extreme, right? It makes you question your instincts, your judgement. You no longer know: what is reasonable? What is needy? You look to the person you most trust for answers. But they have their own agenda.

X told me it was controlling of me to question him getting up at 5 a.m. every day to go to the gym. He told me it was essential for him to stay over at work sometimes. He told me that tracking his iPhone was unforgivable. And that I betrayed his trust. Some of this was true, obviously. Maybe all of it was true? The tracking of your husband's iPhone is not acceptable behaviour. But, at the same time, somewhere I knew that it was the understandable behaviour of a woman whose trust in her husband had been nuked.

We lose our rational self, don't we? I knew somewhere, in the grand scheme of things, that the betrayal of tracking someone's whereabouts would be a petty offence in comparison to the crime against humanity that would be shagging someone else. That would be kind of like starving a dog for days then telling it off for chewing your shoes.

I found myself begging for his forgiveness. Which is fucked up, right?

It was at this point my friend N mentioned the word 'gaslighting'.

Gaslighting, *verb*: to manipulate (someone) by psychological means into doubting their own sanity.

The term gaslighting comes from the 1944 film *Gaslight* with Ingrid Bergman and Charles Boyer, in which Boyer's character slowly manipulates his vulnerable wife into believing that she is going insane in order to distract her from his criminal activities. It's come to mean a particular kind of psychological manipulation, where someone tells another blatant untruths in such a way that they start to believe them and question the evidence of their own eyes and ears. Usually the lies are told with such conviction they become almost unquestionable, partly because you fear the vicious backlash if you do and partly because it sends you further down the spiral of self-doubt. Fiona Murden says, 'Gaslighting eats away at self-esteem and self-belief. The person closest to you is telling lies and that is so difficult and traumatic. It causes you to question your own sanity.'

You might be experiencing a similar thing and not have known that's what it is. Perhaps you are being told you can't shake people's hands (because you do it wrong) or you talk too much at dinner (and embarrass yourself). Both of these scenarios happened to friends of mine. Or maybe when your request to go along to things and meet their friends is repeatedly turned down, you're the one who is being pushy and unreasonable. And because they, the person closest to you, are the one saying it, you believe it. Sort of.

In the same way there is a permanent indent on the finger where my engagement ring used to sit, the pathways in my brain have been wired to trust him.

N.B. A word about the removal of rings. Is there any greater symbol of togetherness than a wedding ring? Or anything more imbued with hope and happiness than a sparkling engagement ring? I can still feel the joy of seeing it glittering on my finger for the first time. Now these rings are a painful reminder of a fairytale smashed, right? If you were married, is yours now on or off? Taking it off is going to hurt. It is an action loaded with pain. So is seeing their finger bare. Plus its absence is going to attract the attention of others. (Think about the *Daily Mail*'s sidebar of shame's next-level scrutiny of celebrities' bare, or otherwise, digits.)

My advice is when you are preparing to take yours off, think about having a rehearsed stock response to people's questions. Stops you spilling your guts and dissolving into snot and tears every time.

To really turn around the situation, I turned the stones in my engagement ring into earrings, which felt seriously good – the sparkles in my lobes giving me a feel-good hit each time I caught a glimpse of them.

Gaslighting is a tactic that's not restricted to romantic relationships. Consider Trump's record of denying proven facts with such authority it makes the truth irrelevant to his fans. Like when he claimed to have 'broken the all-time record for this arena' at his hundredth-day rally in Harrisburg, Pennsylvania, 'maxing out' the capacity while there were, in fact, empty seats.

I went to a retreat once where the yoga teacher gave me a one-to-one. He said he was opening my heart chakra but we both knew he was blatantly touching my boobs. I knew it, he knew it, but he was so brazen it made me question the reality, even as it was happening. And I knew if challenged he would make me feel small.

Adolf Hitler said, 'If you tell a big enough lie and tell it frequently enough, it will be believed.'

A friend of mine spent years feeling shit about herself because she could never get the love she craved from her husband. I watched her slowly diminish, her wattage decreasing day by day. She tried ever more outlandish things to attract his attention but after two years he said he didn't love her in the same way any more and moved out. A whole year later it transpired he had been having an affair all along. For years. With the woman she had questioned him about. Another woman I knew said her husband left her and at the same time her best friend became distant. Both said she was a controlling, paranoid person. They never admitted an affair but 'got together' six months later.

43

In my story X finally moved out, but I still continue to be aghast at how I had chosen to doubt myself rather than question X. I asked Fiona, how do gaslighters justify their behaviour to themselves? She told me the story of one of her friends who is cheating on her husband. The husband, unaware of his wife's affair, is desperately trying to work out the reason for the change in her personality. Meanwhile, she is getting angry that her husband is more possessive and needy and is using that as her justification to continue her trysts.

So how do you navigate gaslighting when it's happening to you? Fiona says, 'If you have anger at being manipulated, then keep hold of it. It helps you keep a degree of sanity.' Then she tells me that trying to get the person to front up to their lies is futile. 'They are trying to protect their own identity, creating their personal narrative. They can't allow that to crumble.' To help deal with it, Fiona suggests being conscious of the gaslighting, writing the stories/lies down, then going through them with a friend or counsellor.

But someone being gaslit wants the liar to face up to the lies! A counsellor or friend seeing the truth is not the same. It's the liar who should be made to feel the full force of their actions. But why? Why is the victim so desperate for them to admit the truth?

Fiona suggests, 'I think somewhere in our brains we think that if they admit the lies they've told, then their whole story will crack open and they will then see the error of their ways. They'll realise they are mistaken and become deeply, abjectly sorry.'

In Fiona's experience do the gaslighters ever admit their lies?

She says it's unlikely. 'Maybe with reflection, over many years.'

So probably not worth waiting for then . . . And what about that weird behaviour when they accuse you of the stuff they are doing? Of not being committed? Or fair? Or being controlling? Or being selfish? 'It's about projecting their own fallibilities onto the other person,' says Fiona. 'It's about protecting themselves. Putting the wrongdoing on the other person.'

If anything is going to make you feel you are losing your mind, it's this stuff. Especially if you didn't see it coming.

My friend Emma told me about 'black swan' events – something that comes as a cataclysmic surprise, has a major effect and is often inappropriately and incorrectly rationalised afterwards, with hindsight. The phrase has been popularised in the book *The Black Swan: The Impact of the Highly Improbable* by Nassim Taleb, who describes how this kind of event is enormously destabilising because it is unexpected and unpredictable. He uses examples such as financial crashes and 9/11, but a personal black swan event is also a thing.

Are sudden cataclysmic break ups worse than a slow agonising demise? Is a body blow worse than death by a thousand cuts? I don't know. Neither is a walk in the park.

I didn't see my break up coming. And it gives me some comfort to say none of my friends or family did either.

Perhaps your break up isn't so dramatic. But even if there was no commandment broken (well, apart from thou shalt not be a flakey nobhead who one minute is talking babies and kitchen worktops but now wants 'space') it doesn't detract from your pain. Or diminish it. Maybe your break up is more the kind where they say, after months of mini-breaking, hand-holding and future planning, 'I'm just really busy at work', or 'My life is too complicated at the moment for a relationship', or 'It's morris-dancing season and I really must source some bells'. They may not have shattered your heart but this will still mean you spend months trying to find the 'real' answer for the change in their behaviour from loving to distant. Even if you both mutually decide that it's over, it still means you are facing the abyss. Uncertainty. Dating apps. But whatever form your heartbreak takes, it seems that all of those on the rejected and dumped end of the break up continuum are obsessed with why.

I know I was. I sometimes still am.

Why, why, why, why, why?

Our exes often tell us why. And maybe what they tell us is true and we just don't want to believe it. Or maybe their reason is a steaming pile of excrement they have concocted to save your feelings. Which is marginally better than a steaming pile of excrement that saves their feelings and conveniently avoids a large part of the story: i.e., I just don't feel the same way about you (and I am shagging Sandra from accounts). Whatever – the why becomes all consuming.

China could break the White House firewall and start sending pictures of Trump on the khazi, Brad and Jen could get back together, Boris could get a crew cut and I will still be deconstructing X's last message and trawling the internet for clues, my friends slowly fossilising at the end of their phones, malnourished and dehydrated as I endlessly circle around the reasons WHY.

Why can't we let the why go? There is a reason. Or a few reasons. Firstly, the brain isn't wired to cope with the question. In his book *I Can Mend Your Broken Heart,* Paul McKenna talks about how the unconscious mind stores and runs millions of programmes of automatic behaviour. Essentially, the brain doesn't want to waste energy carefully considering the millions of possible choices we make every single day, so it develops automatic responses that we perform subconsciously. This is good when you have a breakfast buffet and have to decide between the croissants and the shiny hams (erm, zero choice there) but not so good when it comes to heartbreak.

But back to why we can't let go of 'why'. What we are looking for, I realise, is a palatable answer. One that allows us to keep our self-esteem intact. 'He is a narcissist with a commitment problem and an oedipal boob fixation.' That feels like a much better story to tell yourself than, 'He fell out of love with me.' Which can be the hardest to accept, right?

Guy Winch says listen to their story or make up your own.

Listen to their story . . . Sometimes we don't want to hear what they are saying. Here's where our denial can come in.

X kept telling me, 'It's broken.'

I didn't want to hear this. I begged and pleaded with him not to say it.

'You won't listen to me,' he said.

I *couldn't* listen to him.

Sometimes we refuse to hear what they are saying because we fear it will release a tidal wave of pain so forceful we surely won't survive it. When we drop our barriers, agree to get married, have babies, buy houses – or whatever your version of commitment and together foreverness is – it feels like you and your partner enter a pact that means you won't question the commitment you have to each other. And that becomes the foundation on which everything else is built. So to have to face down the dissolution of it is terrifying. For me it was, anyhow.

Psychologist Andrew Marshall thinks this concept of a forever pact is dangerous and destructive. He also says his female clients 'often have moments retrospectively where they realised the man was trying to communicate his unhappiness but it's so horrifying to the woman they push it away. Then the man doesn't pursue it because who wants to have those conversations?'

N.B. My dad and his partner have always treated the future of their relationship as an open question, never a done deal. As a child this made me feel a bit insecure but I can see the value in it now.

Andrew says there are so many myths that surround love:

- That love should be easy and if it's not, there is something wrong with your relationship.
- That love will solve anything.
- That there's someone for you who can make you happy, that love is the solution.

I can see now how dangerous these thoughts are. How they make it easy to bury any unhappiness, to push it down and not admit to it. I can see how I might have shut down any discussion of X's frustrations and malcontent because if we were to question our union, our shared vision of the future, I feared the whole house of cards might come tumbling down.

Andrew then talks to me about why men have affairs.

Is it because we are not sexy, kind, beautiful, clever, interesting or bendy enough? Is it because we have more body hair than is seemly, or that we hadn't 'put out' enough?

Andrew has written a whole book about it, called *Why Men Cheat*, but here is the lowdown. He says there are various things that women don't understand about men. (No shit. Like how they can spend three hours on the loo? And why they give themselves a full body wash with the hot towels at curry houses?) He tells me a lot of men are brought up to 'act and do', but not to think about emotions. 'They are often working on the surface all the time. If a group of girls is together they'll be asking how each other are feeling. The boys will be pushing each other over. This means that when they are not happy, they don't look deeply at why,' says Andrew. 'Instead they find superficial answers.'

The second thing is, he says, men outsource their emotions to women. First their mothers, then their girlfriends or wives. The women do all the emotional work, buy the presents and arrange the social life. It's not unusual for a man to stand up at his wedding and say to his new wife you've made me the happiest man in the world. Society goes along with it: your wife will make you happy. So when they are unhappy whose fault do they think it is?'

Yours.

Not the career crisis, the pressures of family or the existential crisis that is ageing, but YOU.

Often it seems men have affairs to implode the marriage. On purpose. It wasn't a 'moment of madness', it was a case of doing the worst thing possible, subconsciously or consciously, so a relationship cannot be saved. Cannot be repaired. It's their rowboat out of a situation they don't want to be in. 'They don't want to

50

have the conversation about not being happy because they too have been sold the story that love should be easy and that would be a failure, so they don't,' says Andrew. 'And they don't have the emotional capability to do so.'

Andrew thinks this course of action (napalming their established lives) is rarely a success story. Which may give you a degree of comfort. 'The original problem is still not being attended to and instead of addressing it, they've thrown a can of petrol all over the marriage and now it's gone from bad to catastrophically bad.'

Whatever the mode of destruction, some husbands seem fine. In fact, X told me, a month after moving out, that he was really happy. Hearing that was a body blow. I was struggling to make it through each day. I felt like my life was over and he was . . . happy. WTF?

Talking of which, how many of us struggle to believe it when somebody so outwardly content says they've been unhappy for years? I decided, when X said this, that it could not possibly be the case.

I collected evidence to support my argument. We'd had a mini break the month before I saw his phone. Had sex, had dinners, had a nice time.

Oh yes, he was grumpier. Six plates smashed once when he slammed the dishwasher door closed. He became involved in altercations with other drivers and became so irate about some gardening issue that a friend told him not to get his 'huff in a puff'.

A few months before our marriage imploded, I wrote a piece on how my 'puppy dog' husband was increasingly irascible, now resembling a fang-baring German shepherd. I remember being concerned about his behaviour, but not overly so. X was no grumpier than other friends' husbands. Andrew Marshall suggested to me that: 'Puppy-dog kind of men put people first. Probably first their mother, then you. He'll say, "You know most about the kids so I'll go along with what you think." They work hard and provide and then they reach forty and become conscious they're leading the life someone else wants them to live. Then they realise how pissed off they are. So that comes out in grumpiness. Often men come to me after an affair. As I said, men outsource happiness to women and if another woman comes along and says "I'll make you happy", then they jump. Because they don't discuss feelings, rather than renegotiate the contract with the woman they're with, they give the contract to another woman. Instead of asking, "Who am I and what are my values and what do I want to achieve?" they ask, "Do I fancy this girl next to me?"'

However much I am coming to understand why what happened happened, it doesn't stop the pain. It feels so weird, so strange, how a person you have held at night for decades, who has had your back and you theirs, can switch off their feelings towards you.

In Demi Moore's autobiography (brilliantly ghost written by the genius Ariel Levy), she describes looking into Aston Kutcher's eyes at the end of their relationship and seeing that they were 'icy, dead'. Demi said his were no longer the eyes of someone who loved her.

Worse than unfeeling, the person who has left is often angry.

X was irritated by everything.

I ironed his shirts, though I had never ironed his shirts. He became furious I hadn't done them properly and said it was worse than if I hadn't tried. He shouted, he swore. I hung my head and couldn't understand how I'd become this woman. How he'd become this man.

Now I think, but I don't know (how can we ever know?), that X's anger came from shame. Or frustration. Or maybe he was just really pissed off about the arm creases.

This stage was agonising – frantically trying not to look needy while every fibre of your being craves reassurance. Holding it together for your kids, or at work, when you are so consumed with pain it's hard to hold it in your body.

Eventually, I told myself: he doesn't give a shit what I do. He's over it.

There are a few tactics to get you through the hell that this part brings:

Move

I know I've said it before, but raising your heart rate releases a calm-down neurochemical that helps rebalance the brain. No one ever felt worse for exercise. I ran with two friends. Frosty mornings, sunny ones, rain-soaked ones. One foot in front of the other. Literally and metaphorically.

Allow yourself to feel the pain

'Surrender to it,' says Pippa Grange. She's a psychologist who has written a book called *Fear Less: How to Win at Life Without Losing Yourself* and who helped the young and inexperienced England football team reach the semi-finals in the 2018 World Cup. Facing the pain is less frightening than running from it.

Genuinely see your heartbreak as it is

'Yes you did get rejected,' says Pippa, 'but think about how you are successful in many other ways. Ask yourself, what about myself do I love? Who are my deepest connections with?'

Start journaling

Which sounds like something an American teenager should do while lying on her bed with a fluffy pencil in their mouth. Turns out it just means writing down what you are thinking. That sounds less pretentious, I think. It really helps you make sense of your emotions.

Still, there's no sugar-coating it, no rolling this turd in glitter, this part is the pits. But, if you flip it (and you are going to have to get good at this), the only way is up. Hopefully understanding how and why we are feeling so shit makes the denial phase a bit easier to navigate. Remind yourself that recovery isn't linear. You'll go up and down but you're getting through it, even if it doesn't feel like that most days. One day we'll feel a glimmer of hope, the next abject despair. But slowly we will crawl out into the light. The good days will outweigh the bad. We'll be able to get a sense of perspective.

Know you will sometimes lose it. Snot, tears, the works. And sometimes when you are least expecting it. It's important to allow yourself these feelings. But try to resist doing anything you will regret in time. Posting derogatory comments about the size of his member on his Instagram. Fly posting his sorry face around town. If you handle yourself with dignity you will be glad of it. Remember the Michelle Obama quote: 'When they go low, we go high.'

And when you feel alone, remember that others have got through this. I found hearing their stories was the best comfort in the worst times. This one helped me. I hope it does the same for you.

Dear Rosie

Hi. I don't suppose you manage to read all your emails so if this ends up in spam so be it, but I felt compelled to write as I was very moved by your recent articles about the end of your marriage and how you have managed the situation.

The feelings you describe are exactly how I have felt in a similar situation and I wanted to say you are not alone and thank you for speaking so honestly, it's helpful to other people, it really is!

My husband of fifteen years moved myself and my son to Singapore for his work. We left our whole lives; I left my job, friends, home, etc. Four months later, he ended our marriage and was having an affair with my best friend over there (his work colleague's wife). He became extremely abusive and we had to flee the country and return to the UK with a suitcase just over a year ago now. I've returned to my hometown, not where we lived before, and sought refuge with my parents.

It's been the worst period of my life in so many ways, surviving financially (wealthy husband not giving any money), managing my now twelve-year-old son's emotions, trying and sometimes failing to keep a handle on my own, getting a job and maintaining some kind of professional demeanour while crumbling inside, managing a heinous divorce, nar-

cissistic husband. It's undeniably crappy and my husband has left the building, moved on/in with the new woman, her kids, in our marital bed, the levels of hurt, betrayal and cruelty are unquantifiable.

But, you are right, there are also fantastic people around who have picked me up, dusted me down, shown kindness and understanding and taken us under their wing while we try and heal and 'move on' (don't you love that phrase!).

Anyway, I just wanted to say I'm sorry about what you've gone through, but it makes us all feel stronger to see someone more than managing a horrible situation with aplomb and even humour, so thank you. I'm spending the first Christmas without my son, which is yet another layer of pain, but I'm OK, a glass of Baileys and friends help, I find.

Love,

Lizzy

HEARTWORK

Books to read:

Runaway Husbands: The Abandoned Wife's Guide to Recovery and Renewal by Vikki Stark

The author, a therapist, had been married for twenty-one years when her husband announced one night 'it's over'. He had never said he was unhappy. The author had the kind of marriage her friends were jealous of.

When she spoke about her experience, she found other people were going through the same things. They had reasons to leave like, 'You have a bad knee and I like to go hiking'. Vikki says 95 per cent of men were already in another relationship and often show no remorse.

It's Called a Breakup Because It's Broken: The Smart Girl's Breakup Buddy **by Greg Behrendt and Amiira Ruotola-Behrendt**

If you are struggling to come to terms with the end of your relationship, then this shows you that this shit happens to most people, it doesn't mean you are a loser. The book makes you laugh (really) and calls you out on bad/stalkery behaviour. You will feel better by the end of it.

Know this

The rise in cortisol – which is the stress hormone flooding your body right now – means your coping mechanisms are reduced, and stuff that might have stressed you a bit before can now blindside you. So be kind to yourself. Try and avoid situations that will increase your anxiety levels. Nicky Clinch advises to 'make your world small'.

CHAPTER THREE

Fear and Bargaining ('please don't beg')

'Don't fucking touch your hair'
ALEXA CHUNG, *STYLIST*, 2013

What are you willing to sacrifice to keep your relationship?

Your health?

Your kids' happiness?

Your finances?

Your self-worth?

Your standards?

Your dignity?

Trying to keep someone in a relationship when they want out is a desperation like no other. You find yourself scrabbling to create some kind of connection – even an argument is better than being ignored. Your body craves a look, a gentle touch, kind words. Anything that will ease the pain.

X oscillated between telling me he was committed to making it work, then telling me it was broken.

'Don't be too needy,' said the counsellor.

'Let him feel the draught,' said my friends.

'Have some self-respect,' said my inner voice.

X said his main reason for leaving is that I am controlling. I hadn't heard him use that word before. *Was* I controlling?

I know there is a grain of truth here. I had always been so confident that my choice of paint colour/school for the kids/holiday destination was right. I'd always made the social plans. But did that make me controlling?

See? Headfuck. Are you the things your ex says you are?

I tried to act like I was cool with the fact that he was at best indifferent and at worst 100 per cent over our marriage and asked nothing from him. No reassurance. No help. No kindness. Even though I was dying inside.

You must know the feeling. It takes every ounce of strength not to call them a thousand times. Not to find a reason to be near their office and 'drop in'. Not to try and grab their hand. Or hold them tight.

And the waiting. This is the worst.

When X was due to get the train home I waited, waited, waited for the message to tell me whether he was coming back or not. Like a defendant awaiting a verdict. I was often so tense I found nail marks in my palms hours later. I sat at friends' houses, I went for runs, anything to distract me from the agony. I felt restless and agitated, like I'd been turned inside out.

Sometimes he came home. Sometimes he didn't.

When we are feeling most desperate we look to Google for answers, don't we? Which is never good. I found some 'advice' on the internet that promised 'to turn your marriage around'. It had some enthusiastic reviews and was reassuringly prescriptive. Yes! I thought. A well-reasoned, evidence-based strategy. It absolutely made total sense. At least, it did if your rational mind had left the building, as mine had.

There was an exhaustive list of things you had to do to get your man back and they were all the exact opposite of the things I was doing. Reams of heartbroken women in the comments attested to the success of such an action plan, while scores of others appeared to struggle with how hard it was. The unhappiness and desperation emanated from the screen. I recognised it because I saw it in myself.

The advice was simple but also impossible. Basically you need to resist:

- Chasing them or begging them to stay (er, OK. How?).
- Calling them (and yet this felt like a compulsion along the lines of scratching a mosquito bite).
- Calling their work colleagues (I did manage to avoid this).
- Calling their family.

- Asking for reassurances (pretty much constantly).
- Creating future arrangements.
- Following them around.
- Telling them you love them (all the time. I mean, what was I, insane? OK don't answer that).

Then there was the advice thrown in by a woman who 'won her husband back': 'Don't pursue reason'.

Do. Not. Pursue. Reason. I mean, WTAF?

I knew all about not pursuing reason. Perhaps you, too, have got so desperate that you've succumbed to magical thinking. Magical thinking being all those crazy superstitions we all fall victim to at our most vulnerable. I did A LOT of this. 'If I see two magpies it's lucky, so then we will get through this.' Ditto if the black cat crosses our path. And if I get my hair blowdried or I show him how desired I am by his best friend/boss/favourite barista then he will fall back in love with me. OK, the last one isn't magical, it's just wishful.

But, even so, I knew somewhere deep down that the advice to let go of reason in order to save your marriage is wrong. Very wrong. I knew, on some level at least, that real strength is in telling them to FRO (fuck right off).

That it is not acceptable for me to do 95 per cent of the looking after the kids.

That's it's not acceptable for him to come home after three days AWOL and for his first comment to be that the house is a tip.

Have you begged? I have.

It was humiliating. It was my nadir. The first time it happened was when I came back from a friend's house, where I'd been for a birthday dinner. I didn't want to go because the only time I felt OK was when I was close to him. He didn't want me close to him. It would have been funny if it wasn't so tragic. When I got home, he had gone to bed in the spare room. We had never, ever slept in separate beds. Not in the twenty-six years we had been together. I pleaded with him to come back. He was cold and angry. He wanted space. I couldn't deal with that, so I climbed in with him. He went downstairs to the sofa and I followed him there, like a dog.

'Please tell me you love me,' I begged him, any game face dissolved in an acid bath of desperation. He turned his back on me.

What lengths will you go to in order to keep the status quo? Live in a loveless, sexless marriage? Accept being belittled? Or ignored? Allow your pain to be minimised?

N.B. A word on minimising. I felt like my whole world was falling apart. Because my whole world was sodding falling apart, but X was acting like I should just get over it. That I should continue to function normally. That because this happened to

'50 per cent of couples' it made it OK. By minimising what he was doing, X was making it less bad for himself. If there was no blood then there was no foul, right? It's a classic behaviour by those who need to be able to justify actions that go against their core values. But this messed with my brain. Majorly. Are my feelings of hurt, anguish, devastation overly dramatic? Am I too sensitive?

At the suggestion of the marriage counsellor, I arranged a family trip to the cinema. All of us together, watching a film that focused on the importance of kindness and togetherness. But instead of enjoying the film, I was tense, hoping for any recognition, any softness in X's eyes. I saw nothing. Afterwards, we went to Pizza Express. It was full of happy families chowing down on La Reines and toddlers splattering dough balls in a two-metre radius. X went to the toilet and was gone for an interminably long time. His What'sApp said he was online.

When he came back, I didn't ask why he had been so long. I didn't want to be controlling, after all. I felt sick. And so desperate.

A word on marriage counselling. We went, but – no spoiler alert necessary – it didn't work. Because, I think, X's mind was already made up. I read a quote from a therapist who says that therapy can fix 'everything but contempt'. And it occurred to me that this is where we were – our relationship was being held in contempt.

He decided that I spent too freely and judged too harshly. He was cross that I vetoed his idea of putting matting down in the garden. He said we should have never got back together when we broke up in our early twenties. I felt as if he actively disliked me.

Contempt. Can you see it in their eyes?

For a while, I couldn't believe that X felt so repulsed by me. That he rejected so many of the ideals I thought we shared. I started to believe he loathed me. It was almost like a switch had been flipped and he was suddenly looking at me through new eyes. Perhaps he felt like he was free thinking for the first time in decades. I just felt like he was an entirely new person. I kept searching his face for any glimmer of his old self.

How do you lose perspective on what is acceptable behaviour from the person you love? Have you got so desperate that you've prayed to gods you don't believe in?

How does this desperation affect you physically? Heart palpitations? Headaches? Shaking? Hair coming out in clumps? For me, it was all of these, and I lost weight, dramatically. The medics call it trauma accelerated weight loss. I called it being in a permanent state of flight or flight. So full of despair I couldn't eat or drink. Your body doesn't want to be weighed down with food. It's processing enough. It's primed for battle. Your heart races all day. At night you sleep fitfully and wake up cold, covered in damp sweat.

One morning, a few months in, I decided to get on the scales. The old me would only ever have done this in the morning, having not eaten anything for twelve hours and having been to the bathroom first. I looked down at the dial. 8st 2lb. This is twenty-six pounds below my usual weight of 10st.

I interviewed Liz Hurley, who I'd met before through work. She said, 'You've lost weight. You look great.' (In fairness to her I had put a stone of it back on by then.) There are some pluses to heartbreak. Though this is an extreme way to fit into sample size.

My knickers were baggy, sliding down my emaciated body. My arse looked like a deflated balloon. My bras had become pointless. Even my running leggings flapped around my Twiglet legs. Food tasted like cement.

It is not politically correct to say so but a part of me liked my new body. My frail state meant that people wanted to take care of me. And my skinny wrists and protruding clavicles seemed to be the only arrow that could pierce my husband's hardening heart.

'Green,' said my BFF, visibly shocked. 'We need to put you on a fucking drip.'

Many of my friends, after some alcohol, admitted they were just a teeny bit jealous. An old colleague and friend – who as a health writer had just written a whole run of features about body positivity – laughed and expressed envy. But really, existing in such a state robs you of your power. You can't function when you are so undernourished, when your immune system is depleted. It's the opposite of strong.

Bobbi Brown, beauty entrepreneur turned nutrition guru and supplement queen, told me food plays a vital role in heartbreak recovery. 'I know the last thing you are thinking about is "how am I going to nourish myself?" Often when you're heartbroken you either eat six pints of ice cream or you can't eat a thing. But I truly believe you can't feel better if you are putting junk into your body.'

Word to the wise, listen to Bobbi. Junk food is no good for your skin, your hair or your gut. Your gut is responsible for producing many of the feel-good hormones and God knows these feel depleted when your heart is in pieces. According to a piece written for the American Psychological Society by a Dr Carpenter, 95 per cent of serotonin is produced in the gut, so it makes sense to keep it happy with a good diet. If the idea of eating is repellent right now, think of it like taking medicine – something you've got to do to get better and put this crap feeling behind you.

Bobbi's suggestion was to try bone broth. 'If you feel you can't eat anything, then try this. Just sip on it. It has protein, it has collagen, it's full of goodness. It's a no brainer.'

Sadly bone broth is a one-way ticket to vomville for me. So Bobbi sent me her recipe for a heartbreak smoothie. Because when food is hard to stomach, this is an easy way of getting a hit of nourishment.

I made her smoothie, or a version of it, every week or so. And when I did it gave me a tiny, at first almost imperceptible, feeling of calm. The action of doing it. The taste of it. A small shot of satisfaction that I was looking after myself. That I was working towards a stronger self. It felt the same when I poured some aromatherapy oil in the bath. When I climbed into a hot water bottle-warmed bed. Small, small steps. I am worthy.

You don't have to follow the recipe below to the letter – use whatever you have available – the important thing is you are investing in you.

Heartbreak Smoothie

The ingredients:
Handful of frozen kale – just enough to give it a virtuous green colour
1 scoop chocolate whey protein
Handful of chia seeds – they deliver antioxidants, protein and omega-3 fatty acids.
Frozen cherries
1 fig – I like a little sweetness
1 scoop of collagen powder – it helps to repair and rebuild the skin (Bobbi uses her own brand)
Ice
A slug of nut milk

Rather than being unable to eat, you might be going the other way. Comfort eating. Finding solace in the Dunkin Donuts. That hit of sugar temporarily taking the edge off the pain. Think Elle Woods mainlining chocolate post being dumped by Warner Huntington III in *Legally Blonde*. Or Bridget Jones processing the hurt with a tub of Ben & Jerry's under the duvet. But we all know that neither is great. Perhaps this is the time for us to step away from the fridge and analyse our feelings. How much of our pain is related to losing our partner? How much of the angst and despair is about losing control? Losing our safety net? Losing our vision of the future?

FEAR

My sweat smelt different.

Not the salty, musky comfortingly familiar locker-room smell but instead acrid and sour. When I started looking into this, it turned out the sweat that comes from being scared is different from the usual kind you get when you've gone for it in a spin class. Your apocrine glands are activated when you're under psychological stress. This acrid fear sweat produces a strong, sometimes even sulphurous, odour when you're anxious or scared and it's not just something we can smell on ourselves, others can unconsciously detect whether someone is stressed or scared simply by the odour. Nice. And this stuff makes mincemeat of deodorant.

'A lot of pain comes from fear,' says Dr Pippa Grange. And so this is a good moment to ask yourself, what fears do you have right now? We talk about 'fear' like it's a monolith but there are all sorts of different fears competing for our attention as a relationship falls apart.

Pippa talks about the 'in the moment fear'. In a break up, this might mean 'How am I going to pay the mortgage?', or 'How am I going to manage with the kids?'. These are 'rational fears'. Then there is the fear of the unknown. The swirling 3 a.m. thoughts of 'Will I ever be happy again? Will I lose my mind? Will I die alone and be discovered days, months, later, my body ravaged by rats? Will I be able to live in this house? Will I lose mutual friends?'.

Pippa explains the difference between old fears and new fears. New fears you can rationalise, reason with and reflect on. Such as, 'How will I cope with the house on my own?', or 'Who will get custody of the dog/toaster/electric blanket?'. By contrast, the old fears come from our childhood, from fear centres that exist in our vast unconsciousness – where we have no idea of why we feel the way we do. Pippa talks about an evolutionary fear of abandonment: 'A human child is the most vulnerable infant of any kind of mammal – they are utterly dependent on their parent.' Human children are needier for a lot longer than other species and so that fear of abandonment is programmed into us in an evolutionary sense.

'The root of all our fear, is being abandoned', says Pippa. 'Which is why heartbreak is very taxing.' And if you had a parent leave in your childhood, it means that your abandonment fear response to being left is turned up to mega volume (that'll be me, then). It taps into 'old circuitry' formed in your brain when you were a child, before you were even able to make meaning of what was happening.

But the fact that this abandonment pain is primal and deep-rooted does not mean you're stuck with it. I read voraciously on how to expel it and how to expedite it. There are the usual Google lists of 'how to get over them in a weekend', but sensible advice seems to be you need to 'sit' with the pain and really feel it.

Deliberately feel it? I'd rather get a root canal. But I'm desperate so I'll try anything.

So lie on your bed. Think about how you feel. Dwell. Wallow. You know, all that stuff we are told not to do because it doesn't fit into our 'strong independent woman who is moving on' narrative. Pippa disagrees with that approach wholeheartedly. 'The pain itself is part of the healing. To try to quickly move on, to cover up and fix and make it OK can sometimes really risk true healing. To surrender to the pain and to truly allow the heartbreak sounds so counter intuitive, but you have to allow the pain to roll in so it can roll out.'

It's human to want heartbreak to go away quickly. Perhaps, like me, you take the approach that has always previously meant success in work and in life. Fast forwarding what you want by employing all your mental skills, reading, researching then showing tenacity and determination. Well, I've learnt that you can make it a better recovery, up your odds of happiness and contentment and a more successful second relationship by doing all those things, but by rushing it you run the risk of papering over the cracks.

I remember reading something Nicole Kidman said about her split from Tom Cruise. She said that she wanted the heartbreak to be over straight away; she wanted to short circuit the emotions and drove herself insane with 'if onlys'. Afterwards, she realised that accepting her sad and difficult emotions would have got her over the situation faster than running away from all of those feelings for so long.

How can we help ourselves in this stage, though?

'Telling your truth is powerful,' says Pippa. Talk it out with friends, with professionals, with whoever you find helpful. She also suggests writing or drawing – just getting your feelings out.

I knew I should journal (verb: to write down your feelings with the aim of making sense of them) but I didn't. But I am a career writer, so I write all the time anyway. And I found it extremely cathartic and illuminating putting words on the page in pieces about heartbreak for magazines, which may or may not count. My friend G does journal properly though, and swears by it as a way of clarifying and ordering her thoughts. Something about the time taken to pen them down

72

and the act of committing them to paper makes your brain really feel like it's processing things.

While I was feeling guilty about not journaling, Pippa told me about the Japanese concept of *kintsugi*. It's the art of putting a broken piece of pottery back together by gluing the break with gold. The flaw becomes part of a more beautiful whole. It's become a metaphor for becoming stronger, more resilient, and more appealing from having been smashed apart. The idea that a break up makes you more than, not less than you were before is a comforting thought, right? That the new you that emerges can be more beautiful because of your scars.

Slowly you need to find your boundaries.

You need to find your strength.

I had all but lost my strength in the fear and bargaining and magical thinking. But a flash of it came back at Christmas. I was still hoping for a miracle. Hoping that we would go and get the tree together. That we could be a family. That we could survive this. That the kids' security wouldn't have to be smashed apart.

Then, on 22 December, X told me it was over for good. But he said we should still have Christmas at home for the kids. And his mum and dad. I can't do it, I told him. He told me I was selfish.

Am I selfish, I thought? Should I have the fake Christmas for everyone else's sake but my own?

NO.

This was a major turning point for me. I had known X had been talking BS but this was one step too far. He was leaving me, blowing up my life, blowing up the kids' lives, and yet I was to blame? Before, when he said outrageous things I didn't challenge him because I thought if I did he would walk out. Well, I realised that day, he was going to walk out anyway.

In that moment something clicked. I felt a strength. A certainty. A clarity. Up until that point, I was invested in making it work. Putting every ounce of strength I had into it. Now I was set on survival. For myself. For my children. And that survival meant looking after me, not playing nice and talking about the relative merits of goose fat over sunflower oil for roast potatoes with my mother-in-law while dying inside.

I had found my limit. My boundary. The point at which I could go no further. The flip side to this was I had to give up hope. I had to accept that our marriage was over. That we would not raise our children together. That he would lead a life separate to me. That I would never again hug him. Never rest my head on his chest. It physically hurt.

I decided to take the kids to my cousin Pete's in Devon, throwing everything into the car as fast as I could before I could change my mind. X didn't try to change my mind. He watched as we pulled away. We all sobbed. Me, my mother, the children.

I won't ever know if he sobbed.

You will find your strength. You will be that pot. Stronger and more beautiful for having been broken apart.

Hi Rosie

I want to share my story of heartbreak to see if you and others – if you think it right to share – can help me see my way out of this pain and anger I'm feeling right now.

I've been with my husband for eighteen years, married ten next month, and I've recently found out he's been having an affair with someone at work. I'd suspected it for a while, not least because last September I received an anonymous letter sent to my work informing me he was having an affair with her but giving no further details.

I challenged him at the time of receiving the letter and also insisted on speaking to her but they both vehemently denied it. I said it was his 'out' – we hadn't been happy in a while and I was spending every weekend a hundred miles from our house, looking after my father who was in hospital and couldn't be moved into a care home. Stupidly, I believed his lies but never fully believed that theirs 'was just a friendship', as he told me whenever I questioned him about it. (In fact, he always made it seem like I was the crazy one for thinking that way.)

I finally found the evidence I needed in the form of a Trip Advisor review last June. Unbelievably, he'd snuck off to Cyprus with her for four nights just after lockdown eased, telling me he was going alone to relax. My initial response was to kick him out and file for divorce but of course now he's so sorry, he got caught up in a web of lies and didn't know how to end it. He now wants to focus on us and get back to being a better person and a good husband. He has finished things with her, doing what I asked in terms of getting a STD check and setting up an appointment with a therapist, who we intend to then see together to help us talk things through.

My emotions are all over the place. One minute I'm so angry with them both and cannot feel anything but hate towards them. The next I wonder if he and I can make things better again, if he does what he says he'll do in leaving his workplace and moving to the countryside – something I've been wanting to do for a while.

I am able to take some responsibility for the breakdown of our marriage as I can see where things started to go wrong but I don't think I can get over his intimacy with someone else and all the lies he's told. Especially at a time when I was going through such pain and turmoil with my father being so ill and so far away.

I hate feeling so angry and hurt, and I'm not sure whether to stick to my guns and leave or try to work things out for the sake of what was once a good relationship. I don't think I could ever trust him again and I worry that I'd just put myself through many more years of hell trying.

I know I'll be OK without him as we've always had an independent marriage, but I love him. I love him, but I really hate him right now.

*How do I move forward? Any help and advice is much
appreciated.*
Many thanks,
Vicky

HEARTWORK

Books to read:

***The Unexpected Joy of Being Single* by Catherine Gray**
I wasn't single by choice but this forced me to find the
upsides to being on my own. She doesn't trot out all
the usual shizzle about sleeping star-shaped but instead
makes the case for you completing you. She celebrates
the fact you are free to make your own decisions. Free
to OD on fairy lights and eat what you want for dinner.
Which is, in my case, often muesli.

***How to Fail: Everything I've Ever Learned from Things
Going Wrong* by Elizabeth Day**
Elizabeth Day is clever (Cambridge), beautiful and
successful (journalist) but she describes a life of failures.
One of those being her marriage. It makes me feel A
LOT better that someone like her also struggles in love.
Her insight into human behaviour is breathtaking.

A word about haircuts

I'm not one for laying down the law about heart-break, except for this one: I insist you do nothing drastic to your hair at this stage. If it goes wrong you have two things to sob about – you've been dumped AND you have a haircut that makes you look like a bowling ball with a wig on it. Alexa Chung says it best: 'It's the first thing women do, but you're not in a fit state to make decisions that are long-term – you'll have to spend the next four years growing it out,' she told *Stylist*. 'Don't have a fringe cut. Don't bleach it. Don't do anything, because you will regret it. Buy a lipstick instead. Go and kiss loads of other people, but don't fucking touch your hair, as you'll still feel sad – and you'll have weird hair.'

Hypnotherapist Malminder Gill suggests, 'Get your phone out and record all the gory details of your split. How it made you feel, your deepest fears. Let it flow out of your unconscious mind. Aim for about ten minutes. Then do it again and again. Until the fear gets less. You might need four or five attempts and the recordings will get shorter.'

I've tried this and it helps. Like writing it down, repeating the story and how it all made you feel takes the potency out of the situation. It makes you feel calmer and more rational.

CHAPTER FOUR

Anger
(fury is your friend)

'Even Jesus said adultery was wrong'

Are you angry? Scratch that, are you fucking furious? Are you incandescent that someone has betrayed your trust? Apoplectic that they have broken your heart? Spewing bile at the empty promises and lies? Enraged they robbed you of the future you wanted?

Well, you're not alone. Playwright William Congreve wrote, all the way back in the seventeenth century:

Heav'n has no Rage, like love to hatred turn'd,
Nor Hell a fury, like a woman scorn'd.

It's like a Restoration description of Glenn Close in *Fatal Attraction*. And if your partner has cheated, it's the one time society gives you full licence to be spitting mad, to seek out revenge, to resort to physical violence. You've got the all clear on cutting up the Paul Smith suit they so fucking fancied themselves in, slashing their tyres, social media shaming them, fly postering their cheating face round town, emptying the bank account. Hell, you can send out a sodding press release listing their misdemeanours and everyone would back slap you and say, 'You go, girl.'

It's the stuff of movies.

'Don't get mad, get everything,' said Ivana Trump in *The First Wives Club*. And people in the cinema actually clapped.

Thou shalt not commit adultery. Even Jesus, Mr Forgiveness himself, said it was wrong.

I recently read a 2020 Ipsos study on British morality, which mirrored one done in 1989. It showed that, while as a society we have become less critical about many things (for instance, back then, 49 per cent of people thought homosexuality was wrong and in 2020 that number has dropped to 36 per cent), the only area in which tolerance has decreased is infidelity. In 1989, 52 per cent of people felt infidelity was morally wrong. Today that percentage has increased to 55 per cent.

X and I used to talk about what we would do should infidelity occur between us. Or actually, should I do such a thing because it was so unthinkable he might be the one to cheat. He would say he would maim the man, talking about various revenge scenarios which involved Tarantino-levels of blood and gore. And though I'm generally violence averse (I find it hard to watch David Attenborough – those gazelles get me every time) his passion felt good. Though I did point out that a father serving time for grievous bodily harm was possibly not beneficial for the children. I found his passionate fury weirdly romantic in that it showed the depth of his love for me. Although, in retrospect, it could be seen more that he thought of it as an ownership issue.

As a teenager and twentysomething, you are pretty clear on lots of things. Your position on Radio 4 (boring). Ditto country walks, picturesque views and gardening. Oh, and if your partner ever cheats he'd be out on his ass. That goes for your partner being rude, or disrespectful, or seriously inconsiderate, right?

But that is before you get married, before you have kids, before your friends and finances become so intertwined that unpicking them is unimaginable.

At our wedding, we had a quote from the novel *Captain Corelli's Mandolin* by Louis de Bernières (along with every other couple in the noughties). My friend Fi stood in the pulpit and talked about 'roots that grew towards each other underground, and when all the pretty blossom had fallen from our branches, we found that we were one tree and not two'. I felt that to sever our shared roots would surely result in, if not my death, then something approaching it. I wasn't sure I could survive the separation.

Our reactions are not what we think they are going to be. Not the movie version.

81

Faced with rejection and disrespect, I hoped I'd be fiery and resolute. Eyes glinting, body shaking with fury. I wanted to be wild and spitting mad. Think Penelope Cruz in *Vicky Cristina Barcelona* with a gun and good hair.

What I wasn't expecting was X's anger.

He was furious. Red-faced, clenched-fist furious. Which was a headfuck, because surely anger was my right and privilege as the spurned spouse?

N.B. I now hate the word spouse. It's like when you give birth and all the doctors call you 'mum' and you realise your entire identity has been compart-mentalised into one role. You never, ever get called 'spouse' unless you are divorcing.

X was furious about everything as our relationship crumbled. Furious that, in his eyes, I had overspent and under contributed. Furious about bad dishwasher stacking. I had never seen his anger at such intensity and it scared me. X was so angry it felt like he'd got the monopoly on it. I found myself in the role of the placater, but I couldn't placate him. I was walking on eggshells. Trying to manage and dampen down any blow up. The more angry he got, the more submissive and pleading I became. My anger could never match his, so I gave up trying. I shrank from it. Made myself smaller. Why, why is the person who is leaving, the person who has smashed the marriage, so angry? How can they be so mad at the person they have lived so much of their life with? Even if they don't love us now, surely they still feel empathy for us? Surely they look at their heartbroken partner and feel pity at least?

It doesn't seem like it.

Why?

'They hate themselves' is the common response. Makes sense, if you know you have done something dubious – nicked a parking space, jumped the queue, got a speeding ticket – when questioned you become angry, right? Righteous. Anger masks feelings of inadequacy, protects the ego and makes your actions that bit more palatable. To yourself, at least. In your eyes, it helps exonerate you from wrongdoing.

Plus, if your ex cheated, or behaved badly in another way, they know you, rather than they, have the clean sheet, so they resent you for that. And they can't allow themselves to feel empathy because if they do, then they will have to face up to their wrongdoing.

X seemed so absolute in his vision of the truth that it made me question mine even more. You need strength to be angry.

Do you have any?

Were you fiery?

Are you fiery now?

I was always feisty. Take no shit. Fully aware of my worth. But I think having children makes any woman more aware of her vulnerability. The power balance gets shifted. Which is biological, right? Suddenly you are so much more dependent on your partner, for help, for money, for support.

And so it was that my violence towards X was limited to that punch on that first day. Within minutes, as we stood together in the garden, my brain had taken over my emotions. I was in deep shock. I remember that sick, strange, all-consuming feeling that this was very, very bad. Life-alteringly bad. The enormity of it pressing up against my brain like storm water against a dam.

But still, even as my mind scrambled to comprehend the incomprehensible, I was able to rationalise. To strategise. To know that I could not, and would not, let my life blow up. The life I had worked so hard to create. Even with a million feelings coursing through my veins, I knew the main one was fear. Fear that life as we knew it would be shattered into a million different pieces, each shard with the potential to lacerate and wreak devastation, if I let it. So even as the pain and panic ran through my veins, I knew I had to fight for safety and security, for my children and myself. X was the only safe harbour I'd ever known. I couldn't imagine a life where he wasn't there, the yin to my yang.

I loved him.

It strikes me that up until now I haven't talked about my love for X. Maybe because it's too painful, too much for my ego to take. Or maybe it's because, more than him, I loved the idea of him. The idea of a family unit. The idea of a secure future. But I did love him. I loved his strong, capable body. His uncomplicated attitude to life and relationships. I loved his face, with his straight, masculine nose, his square jaw. I loved that he knew how to wire a plug, how to wallpaper a wall. I loved that he was so appreciative of whatever food was laid in front of him, that he was easy company. Quick to smile. That he giggled and loved gossip, though he pretended not to. I loved that he seemed so fiercely family-focused when security and protection was something I had craved so badly as a child.

I couldn't lose this.

So any anger I had was pushed right down by fear. Which meant I wasn't angry. At least, I didn't think so. But in retrospect, I wonder, as women, are we conditioned out of anger? Elizabeth Day once told me, 'As girls, we were raised to be kind and nice.' Boiling rage is unladylike, right? But the psychologists and therapists say some anger is good. Psychologist Andrew Marshall said to me, 'Your husband left you and was horrible, but you are not angry?'

I wished I could feel it.

My friend H, whose story played out similarly to my own, questioned why, when confronted with unreasonable, disrespectful or downright wrong behaviour, neither of us told our respective exes to FRO.

I still grapple with why. I think it's partly because whenever I questioned X's narrative he responded with such aggression and vitriol it messed with my mind.

The backlash was so strong I couldn't bear it. Plus, and I'm only just realising this, I have spent so long peacekeeping that I am now programmed that way. I don't like confrontation. I don't like aggression. A spat with X by text, by phone or in person makes me feel physically sick and shaky for hours. This makes me feel a bit pathetic but it's the truth.

But, despite this, I hope you can feel some anger.

Why? Because some anger is a right and proportion-ate reaction to being treated badly. And Malminder Gill actively encourages it: 'When you are angry you recognise something bad has been done to you. Anger is about self-respect,' she says. 'If you get angry, you are saying "I don't deserve to be treated this way".'

By now, X and I were going to marriage counselling. X didn't want to go, said it was a 'waste of time', said he would not contribute towards the cost. My cousin, who clearly was thinking murderous thoughts about the man he once considered a friend, said he would pay. I paid. For an hour of torture once a week. Why torture? Well perhaps because it had become for me about trying to keep X invested in our marriage – I felt the focus became what I had done wrong, how I was going to correct my mistakes. How I was going to change. I was constantly apologising for my errors. Of course, I accept my behaviour hadn't been perfect but I should have battled my corner. I couldn't. Instead I accepted each criticism, absorbing it like a punching bag.

I came across a piece in *Psychology Today* by Suzanne Lachmann which talks about the successive emotions in a break up. If you imagine a ladder from despair to happiness, at the bottom is fear and denial and then you move up to anger. Anger, according to Suzanne, means 'at the very least there are shades of remembering you matter too, of feeling justified in realising that you deserve more from a relationship'. It's a sign that you're not right at the beginning any more.

So if we don't feel angry at the way we have been treated, does that mean we are not progressing? 'If a human being never shows anger, then I think something's wrong. He's not right in the brain,' said the Dalai Lama. And he knows his shit, right?

I knew I was not being right in the brain. I knew I was cowed. And I hated that about myself and the situation. I wanted, I needed anger.

Pippa Grange recommended to me the author Martha Nussbaum, who wrote a great book called *Monarchy of Fear*. Nussbaum refers to anger as the 'child of fear' and talks about the myth of the 'Furies', ancient goddesses of revenge. The Furies are ugly, twisted, resentful and predatory creatures who dwell in the forest at the edge of a city. They are hidden, dismissed, out of sight but inescapably there. In the story that Nussbaum relates, Athena, the goddess of strategy and wisdom (among other things), doesn't keep the Furies banished in the middle of a crisis, she invites them into the city walls and gives them a voice. Pippa says, 'I think this is good advice for anyone going through heartbreak.'

Because anger is often ugly or explosive, we feel it isn't 'civilised' to show it, or we don't really like who we are while we are showing it. Pippa says that's because: 'We only know how to show anger in particular ways – outbursts, emotional rampage or verbal daggers to the side ribs. I think it's important to honour your anger, express it plainly, calmly and give it voice, rather than allow it to become twisted up and banished, ever ready to leap.' She continues, 'Anger is full of the fear of our own human vulnerability and helplessness. It's obvious why this affects people after they have been rejected in some way. So it's not enough just to honour the anger and state your complaints, you have to also dig down a little further and have a good look at the fear that goes with it. Am I not lovable? Am I not good enough? Honouring the anger also means looking at the fear, and it's the fear you soothe.'

Wow. I hadn't contemplated that there were different types of anger before. And once again, I think it's all about the superpower of self-awareness. About thinking about your reactions to events and what triggers your anger. How your childhood and your relationships have shaped you. And how you can channel your anger to your benefit.

I wanted to get angry. But how do I do it? How do I find the bloody thing? Is it in the laundry basket lurking under my self-esteem? Or buried deep down in my subconscious, next to my fear of sunflower heads?

Getting in touch with our emotions sounds like something Gwyneth Paltrow's vagina steamer would say.

While I was wondering where my anger might be found, the *Telegraph* offered to send me on a 'Tarant retreat' in Italy for a feature. Tarant is an Italian purifying ritual for souls that need help and is based on a centuries-old tradition of midlife women being bitten by a spider, going mad and needing an intervention by their friends. The 2020 lens would say these donnas had got thoroughly fucked off with the domestic drudgery, the invisibility and boredom of their lives, the hormonal upheaval of the menopause, and had to let it all out somehow. But hey, I needed help. I was in.

The retreat was women only and offered the opportunity for 'rebirth' and to be cosseted in the 'twilight womb of the Vair spa'. I had envisaged it being lots of women screaming expletives about their philandering husbands and dancing naked while howling at the moon. However, I arrived to find a very chi chi resort, at which I was met by a team of 'camari'. Camari means female companions and these staff members are there to support your journey, finding the best treatments/ meals and activities for you.

Over the next few days, we danced to the tambourine, played by a man in a dodgy waistcoat (this was a bit much for my British cynicism). You get your hair brushed by an Italian Nonna at night, which was a bit weird but rather nice. Luckily my Nonna couldn't speak English so conversation was limited. We did morning yoga and then there was a Thai massage on a rubbery matt, which involved being oiled, then stretched sixty ways by a shirtless man, pulled into positions that felt verging on indecent. I was glad I was wearing my bikini and not the skimpy paper pants provided. Then there was some weird stuff – like twirling whirling dancing – to exorcise some madness. And there were also more familiar massages and scrubs and amazing food from the organic farms. Which was altogether divine and actually did really help me in my still very fragile state. Just being touched by people, by the sun, helped.

I still hadn't got in touch with my anger, though.

I was crushed that X behaved so disrespectfully, that he turned his back on me and our marriage. But sometimes I felt grateful because it made it easier for me to make him 100 per cent the bad guy. But this is something the genius writer Nora Ephron warns against. If there is a patron saint of women who have survived an extra marital affair, it is Nora. Her husband's affair was a scandal in its day, immortalised in her novel, *Heartburn*. *Heartburn* is one of the greatest books ever written about the dissolution of a marriage. I cannot recommend it highly enough. Nora wisely cautions that if your partner did the ultimate bad deed you can start to view your marriage break up as a one-sided situation. It feels nice. Neat. They are the villain of the piece and you are blameless. It can conveniently wipe out any of your own misdemeanours, absolving you of all guilt. Like the lower-grade sins of greed, bickering or petty jealousy. Or being fucking annoying about the dishwasher stacking.

One of the things I love the most about *Heartburn* is that Nora was so offended about her husband's choice of affair partner. The book was fiction but I think we can assume a certain crossover into reality. She was most peeved that this woman was a 'giant'.

And the other party is something worth thinking about, is it not? For people who have been betrayed, it would seem most dignified to ignore them. But, judging by the stories I have been sent, the interesting thing is the person is often not what you fear. You might imagine that this temptress must have the looks of a supermodel. The brain of a QC. The style of a Parisian. Think Amal Clooney. Your basic fucking nightmare.

Often they are none of those things. Which is reassuring yet also slightly offensive – if he was going to leave, surely it should be for someone spectacular rather than just normal? But your ex obviously sees something in them that they want. Maybe it's about someone less challenging or questioning. Or someone who flatters and fawns. Perhaps they are gentler or harder, or always put all the knives together in the right segment of the dishwasher. (Though if your ex is shagging an Amal Clooney lookalike, I can only send you my sympathies.)

I know that for all the people like me, who can't get in touch with their anger, there are so many who are spitting mad. And it's understandable because, thanks to your ex's choices and their actions, your way of life, your future, your security and your kids' security is shattered. If you are/were married, your ex broke the vows of 'to have and to hold from this day forward'. If they cheated they have broken more of them.

Anyway – back to who is the baddie. It can be tempting, for women who own the moral high ground due to their partner's infidelity, or another reason, to let our anger mask our hurt. To blame the affair partner. To call her names or call her out to her colleagues. But just as we want our exes to address the real feelings that underlie their anger, we need to make sure we do to. Because anger can distract us from dealing with the real injury to our ego. Blaming a cheater helps us not to blame ourselves and stops us feeling like we deserved it or that we weren't lovable enough. But it can also stop us learning and growing.

When I posted about anger on Instagram, the messages came flooding in. One woman said anger fuelled her survival. It made her able to get up every day, to go to work, to keep a roof over her baby's head. Using anger as fuel to your fire seems a common theme. Use it to your advantage. F-you is a powerful motivator, right? I will be OK. I will survive. I will thrive.

Another woman DM'd to say she realised the difference between 'present and past anger'. She uses present anger as a motivator, an engine of change. But past anger, she says, keeps her stuck.

92

Responses to another post on the subject revealed being stuck in anger mode is the number one concern of many people. Possibly because, as divorce coach Sara Davison says, to be continually angry gives your ex control. Sending furious text messages, shouting down the phone, ranting to your friends – it's never going to give you the satisfaction or peace you crave. In fact, it just hurts you more deeply. And it continues your connection with them.

Sara suggests replacing that behaviour with something else. Something positive. Channel the energy away from them and towards you. If you are finding it hard to calm down try Sara Davison's tactics for defusing anger:

1. Punch something not someone. Taking a boxing class might sound like a cliché but it's good for getting the emotion out of your system.
2. Flip it. Yes, it's shit, but find something positive from the negative. Ask yourself, what can I learn from this?
3. Shift your focus. Think about you not them.

Remember, the ultimate sign you are over it is indifference. We know all this, but emotions are hard to wrestle with, right? And false positivity is, well, false. There's fake it till you make it, and then there's lying to yourself. Burying your anger, or any other emotion, is not good. You have to allow yourself time to really think about your heartbreak. To process it. To come up with new strategies for a positive spin on it. And then you can move on.

A famous phrase that I've read in various forms, says that resentment is like 'drinking poison and expecting the other person to die'. Anger can congeal into bitterness and the only person that bitterness harms is yourself. Not to mention that persistent anger means your ex is staying rent free in your head.

I wanted to use the power of my emotions to show that I wouldn't be broken. That I would rise up like a phoenix from the ashes. Of course, X didn't give a crap what I did (as long as it didn't puncture his narrative). But that's beside the point.

Ultimately, there is no right or wrong way to feel.

And if all of the above doesn't help, maybe this statistic will. A study by Baylor College of Medicine in Houston claimed that of men they studied who died during sex, 93 per cent were thought to have been engaging in extra-marital affairs.

Which is a comforting thought, no?

Dear Rosie

I've been following your story and when I saw your Instagram post on anger I had to write.

After sixteen years of marriage, my husband told me he wanted to separate, that he no longer loved me. He moved out a couple of years ago. He consistently denied there was anyone else but I found out a year ago that he had been having an affair for almost a decade. I'd always been suspi-

cious of their friendship but he told me I was paranoid and if I questioned him he would just shut me down.

I am so angry. I feel like he's defrauded me of ten years of my life. I know if I'd uncovered it earlier it would still have hurt like hell but I would have had the power of knowledge. I think withholding that information is the worst thing a person can do.

I haven't really felt anger before. Not like this. I don't think I have an angry nature and I think I have always had a willingness to please men. But when his affair was revealed I was extremely angry. Furious. I threw stuff, I dumped his clothes out. I have been angry every day for six months. It comes over me like a wave. It's physically very uncomfortable. It feels hot. My neck prickles. Sometimes I'll fire off angry texts to him.

But I've also discovered the positives about anger. It helped me distance and detach myself from him. And it gave me a certain energy. A vigorous energy that kind of inflates me. Gives me back some self-worth. But I know I need to limit my ranting about his betrayal to my friends. There's a statute of limitations on friends' patience. Luckily time means my anger is fading.

I've learnt that if you strip anger right back it's anger at yourself. Now I know I will never allow myself to be treated this way again. Anger, or lack of it, led me into the situation and anger led me out again.

Jxx

HEARTWORK

Books to read:

Heartburn by Nora Ephron

If you haven't read any Nora Ephron, I'm jealous that you get to discover her for the first time. She is insightful, witty and feel-good – a legendary chronicler of the female human experience. In this book, she manages to be side-splittingly funny about the pain of her husband's infidelity. The observations are on point and you will feel better for reading it, I promise.

Leave a Cheater, Gain a Life by Tracy Schorn

If your self-belief has been shot to shit by infidelity, you need to read this book. In trying to keep a relationship together, the focus often goes onto the unmet needs of the cheater. Which can mess with your head. This smart, sassy read will help get you back on track.

Things to try

Makeover your place. I know this seems like a big ask when pressing a button on the remote is quite frankly enough of an achievement, but you know all those people asking what they can do to help? They can take down the wedding pictures. And take you to IKEA and buy you some cushions and house plants.

CHAPTER FIVE

Depression
(good grief?)

'Your lowest point is your turning point'

How low can you go? If you're anything like me, this may be the worst you've ever felt. Are you over-whelmed, exhausted, unable to see a way through? In the midst of my split, I couldn't eat, focus or feel anything but abject despair.

I took myself to the doctor for sleeping pills. I felt I needed some sleep to function. And I knew that these pills would give me a few hours respite from the thoughts that tormented me. Constantly. Instead my doctor suggested anti-depressants. She said they would help me sleep and also help me get some clarity of thought. Plus allow me to eat. Allow me to function.

I didn't think I was depressed. Anxious, yes, but depressed?

According to the NHS, depression is defined as 'feeling persistently sad for weeks or months, rather than just a few days'. Which was definitely me. But when is it grief and when is it depression? The distinction is in whether or not the feelings of sadness and loss come and go, in between times when you still enjoy things and look forward to future events (grief) and a constant, all-pervading sadness that feels inescapable (depression). It is so hard to recognise depression when you're in the middle of it − I know I didn't, even though I couldn't find any positives in my life. I couldn't imagine a happy future or dig up any hope. So though I was resistant to taking anti-depressants, I knew I needed help. Above all, I needed to parent.

I was prescribed a low dose of the anti-depressant sertraline. It took about a month to kick in but when it did, I catastrophised less and felt more in control. I felt a shift in my mood. I was more positive. Less overwhelmed.

There is still a stigma around anti-depressants, isn't there? When I posted about them on Instagram I got an amazing response, I think because people feel there is still judgement about them, so were relieved to see me being open. There's still a school of thought among some people that you should just 'pull yourself together' instead. Well, now I know that sometimes you can't. I know anti-depressants aren't for everyone and I'm not trying to push them but I feel it's important to be honest about their role in my recovery. I do think you need to read up on their side effects, though. For me, this was cold sweats and mild stomach problems. But the side effects were far outweighed by the benefits. I do worry about coming off them, though. I tried once and felt pretty – OK, *really* – dreadful.

Perhaps by now you've experienced the lacerating pain of watching your ex walk away with your hopes and dreams, packing up your self-esteem in their holdall/van and taking off.

The immediate drama has subsided. The terrible fights, the desperate pleas, the accusations are over. You've experienced the gut-wrenching moment when they, or you, or both of you, talk about a future without each other. The worst thing that could happen has happened and now you have to deal with the aftermath.

For me the idea was abhorrent. Nausea inducing. It pricked the bubble that I imagined surrounded us. Me, him, the kids. Instantly vaporised that beautiful, iridescent rainbow film that gave me a feeling of safety, security and certainty. That story of togetherness that kept love inside and life's harsh realities out.

Once those words have been uttered, once the pact that you have both willingly entered into has been questioned, it's like the walls are breached and the ugliness floods in. Perhaps because you are no longer complicit in the collusion of together forever, perhaps because you are no longer mirroring each other's behaviour, smoothing off each other's edges, your differences become violently obvious. And the differences in your opinions are suddenly shocking. The coldness and detachment which X displayed was beyond comprehension to me. My desperation and softness obviously irritated him.

Sometimes, perversely, you don't want the bruises to fade. Don't want the rows to stop, the pain to transition from gut wrenching to dull ache, because that would mean facing that it's over.

Newsflash: it is over. Your new reality is being single.

You love them. They don't love you. Or maybe you love the idea of them. Whatever. There's no one to share your concern about the leaking roof. Nobody to massage your shoulders after a stressful day or to make plans for next year, next decade. No one to be concerned if you stumble (literally or figuratively).

Conversely, there's no one to care for – romantically at least. I know there are kids and guinea pigs but there's no one to pick up that nice sweater in the sale for. No one to nurse. No one to cook for. No calls at bedtime to say good night when one of you is away.

Then there's the moment you realise you are a single mother. The moment you are asked for your next of kin and don't know who to say. When you look in the back of your passport and see their name as your emergency contact. Only now you don't know where they live or who they are with. Every day contains a thousand different paper cuts in the form of joint invitations, letters, and those sodding photo memories. Christmas cards with happy families on the front. Having to write your own and there being just three names. Every day there are a million moments when lemon juice is squeezed on your wound.

A new friend emails me. How, she wants to know, do you navigate the following?

1. Listening to friends talking about their family and husbands.
2. Watching TV shows or films with constant references to love, happiness, families.
3. Hearing your kids casually mention something that they've done with your ex and knowing you will never be part of that again or have that family unit again.
4. The high of a trip away/treat/night out and the disproportionate low when returning to reality alone.

I would add to that list solicitors' letters (with lots of repetition of the word 'spouse') that, when they come through the door, make you shake with fear. And interaction with my ex, which was fraught and lacerating. Every time I saw X it would precipitate a maelstrom of emotion. The unpredictability of our encounters was disconcerting.

All I can say is that it feels shit, it is shit, but these things will normalise over time. And if you front up to them, you will get over them more quickly.

Open the scary letter from the lawyer or the bank.

And, as a gazillion self-help books suggest, sit with the pain.

But sitting with the pain sounds weirdly meaningless. I mean, haven't we all been taught that to expedite the achieving of anything (and in this case, happiness) you must push on through and throw all your efforts into meeting your goal? I am not a wallower but a do-er. Because wallowing, with a tub of Ben & Jerry's and a bottle of vodka, seems to me to indicate you are stuck. Not progressing. Not moving forward. No, I decided, I needed to get out there, date, get the body of a supermodel and the career of my dreams.

But is that the right way? Nicky Clinch, a transform-ational life coach, says you can't bury your feelings. Her motto is 'what you resist persists'. Ignoring how you feel doesn't get you through the pain, the pain just stays there waiting for you. If you ignore or repress those painful feelings they will eventually come back and bite you on the ass. Nicky promises, however unlikely it may sound, that 'this time of pain can be a gift, because it forces you to address old wounds, to come out the other side with more self-knowledge, better able to find true contentment'.

But this means you have to do 'the work'. And quite frankly, that did not sound appealing. At this point, after exhausting rows, emotional drama, the months of not sleeping or eating, the idea of more work was daunting. I wondered if I had the energy to do what Nicky advised. To examine my behaviour, my thought

102

processes, to see how the things that have happened in the past make me react the way I do. To unpick how I contributed to the unravelling of my relationship.

Fan–fucking–tastic.

Nicky says many of us have old wounds that inform our behaviour in relationships. Nicky and I both have fathers that left in early childhood. 'If you look at it on a therapeutic level,' she says, 'most big incidents like this that happen in adult life will re-trigger something or reactivate something from our childhood. They will trigger something that's unhealed or on hold from the past.'

I think about my own childhood. How my relationship with my father made me crave solidity and security. It's easy to dismiss the cliché of blaming all of your relationship problems on how you were parented (e.g., 'my dad did not attend my gymnastics prize-giving and thus I have become a man–pleasing exercise addict') but there is no doubt it shapes you. For a long time, I kept any man at a distance, testing them emotionally, pushing them to breaking point to prove the depths of their commitment. I recognise that in choosing X I was choosing safety, but in many other ways we weren't a match. I pushed X out of his comfort zone, often.

I'm not sure if realising this very old childhood pattern makes me feel better but it makes me see that our split is the culmination of so many of our formative experiences and differences in ideals and goals. And not necessarily a rejection of me. Which helps. Even while it hurts.

Pippa Grange says, 'Let the pain roll in, so it can roll out. The pain itself is part of the healing. To try to quickly move on and cover up and fix and make it OK and be positive can sometimes really risk true healing. You need to be able to surrender to the pain and allow the heartbreak.'

Sodding great. As well as dealing with the end of my marriage, I now had to delve deep and look at how shit it felt as a child to have a parent leave. The joy never stops.

My friends wanted me to go to a counsellor. I was reticent. In the midst of my depression, I didn't feel I had the capacity to arrange it, to meet a stranger, to tell them about my messy, embarrassing, verging on pathetic thoughts. How do you find a counsellor even? And how much do they cost?

I looked at Relate. Fuck, it was bleak. The website was full of tales of woe and depressing stories. It told me counsellors range from £30 to £60 and hour. But I know some London ones can go up to £120. In the end I got a recommendation through a friend.

A word about counsellors: many people think therapy is for actors or navel-gazing types who like to talk about chakras and probably ate their placenta post-childbirth. Not for 'normal' people like you and me. We are fine as we are, thank you very much. Just a cup of tea and a biscuit is all we need to sort us out. But counsellors help.

And we could do with that right now, don't you think? But a little bit about the weirdness that is a visit . . .

It's weird not asking them about themselves. It's weird that they don't tell you what to do but try to get you to come to your own conclusions. This can be annoying when you want them to say, 'He's a shit, you should definitely shag his best friend.' But it's probably best in the long run. It's weird that they almost always have suspect sofas that look wipe clean. Unless you go to a really expensive one, in which case they might have an Eames chair. They always have a box of Kleenex. And, according to my mate Jen, who says she's been to them allllll, they are always five per cent smug. But she admits this might just be her take. Just like going to the gym, I think you always feel better once you've been. But it's hard, really hard, hauling your ass there.

My counsellor questioned certain thoughts of mine. That I was incomplete without a man. That my self-worth and happiness depended on a man loving me. That if I was kind/clever/gorgeous enough, then a man would love me even if they were quite blatantly not in a place to have a relationship. She talked to me about where my beliefs came from. Asked me why I had made certain life choices. Discussed the impact of my parents' separation. And there were a few light-bulb moments. Like when I talked about craving the security of a nuclear family as a child so I tried to create it in adult life. Talking about how I felt trapped as a new mother and that built into frustration and resentment.

105

How I would cajole and persuade those around me so I could have things the way I wanted them. How my career in media and women's magazines made me put so much value on looks.

My counsellor also talked to me about boundaries. And there were a few times when she did proffer an opinion and say certain things were not acceptable. Things X did that overstepped the mark. He probably felt there were things I did too. I can't really go into them here but in the later stages of our marriage I would find myself holding back from voicing my concern about X's actions because I couldn't face the vehemence with which he would defend his position. In the later stages, there were things like his refusal to say where he had moved to. When I questioned him on it, he told me I was being pathetic and controlling.

She helped me work through my feelings. But again – what does 'working through your feelings' mean? We hear it said all the time – but how do you actually do it? The way I understand it from my own therapist, working through your feelings means having the self-awareness to look beyond the obvious emotion (hurt, anger, sadness) and see what is at the root of it. Sometimes this is intensely painful which is, I suppose, why a lot of people avoid it.

And yet, despite my misgivings, it helped. With my counsellor, I feel I can be at my most vulnerable. I don't have to protect my ego. I don't have to say I'm fine. I don't have to say this is probably a good thing and I'm better off without him. I don't have to make her like me.

Another good thing about going to a counsellor is that it stops you leaning on your friends so much. Because, while your friends want to help, they see your relationship through the prism of their experience. They will have wise observations and comfort and an endless supply of wine and swear words but they can't help but bring their own baggage to the table, as well as carrying a bit of yours ('Do you remember when he said . . . ?'). They might want to get you back together because they liked how easy that was, and well, they like him. They might hate his guts because their last boyfriend did something similar. Plus, they are human and so they will, eventually, get bored of listening to the pity party. The pros, on the other hand, are trained to be impartial and well paid to listen. They stop you getting stuck in thought patterns that don't serve you.

But this is not to say I'm not desperate to leave at the end of each session. Checking my watch surreptitiously to see if my fifty-five minutes is up. Does this count as sitting with the pain?

When do you feel the pain? At night? In the morning? Sometimes it helps to identify when you're most likely to be hit by the most painful thoughts so that you can prepare yourself a little. And forgive yourself when it happens. You can tell yourself that they will pass. That while you feel turdy today, you may well feel hopeful tomorrow.

The time when I really felt the pain was when I was driving alone. There was nothing to distract me. I couldn't call anyone. I couldn't look at Instagram. Or my emails. Or my WhatsApp messages. The songs on the radio seemed to have a direct line to my heart. It was then that the pain burnt and the sadness was inescapable. The tears would come. The nightmarish scenes replayed over and over in my head. Is this supposed to be helpful? It felt crap. There was nothing exquisite in the pain. But the opposite is denying the pain exists. Glossing over it. Pretending you are fine.

I was sent by my editor to Viva Mayr, an Austrian detox clinic where the celebs go to lose pounds and give their guts a break. By not eating any food. A week here costs the equivalent of a small car. Luckily I got it gratis as I was reviewing it for work.

I went with my friend Nadine, who is an anti-depressant in human form. Even though I felt pretty shit when I arrived – with a contraband bag of ready salted crisps – her wicked sense of humour made me feel a lot better before any treatments had even begun. Our rooms overlooked a startlingly blue lake. The place had a starched white clinical vibe. You feel very looked after in a brisk Austrian-type way. We lay on sun loungers on the jetty and watched as the have-yachts in fluffy bath robes took important business calls. Despite the luxury surroundings, I was still overwhelmed with sadness and full of fear.

In desperation, I had signed up for emotional healing with a Viva Mayr psychotherapist called Claudia Kohla. A no-nonsense maternal figure, she asked me to lie on a treatment bed and relive the worst moments of my break up. She uses a type of psychotherapy called EMDR (eye movement desensitisation and reprocessing). It's based on rapid eye movements, which connect to emotional trauma. The technique is often used to treat PTSD. The therapist asks you to recall distressing events. In my case, that meant asking me to think of all the awful moments of my split and the emotions that went with it. Claudia asked me to follow her fingers with my eyes. She moved them from side to side and then she tapped my body. The tears came and, because I was lying down, they streamed down my face and pooled into my ears. Which was a new sensation for me. She then got me to think of more pleasant memories. Which was a relief.

The idea of EMDR is that you take the intensity out of those traumatic memories. It works by getting you to relive traumatic or triggering experiences in brief doses, while the therapist directs your eye movements. The theory being that recalling distressing events is often less emotionally upsetting when your attention is diverted.

Did it work? Well, afterwards I felt shaken and exposed. I felt the raw grief more keenly than I had for a while. It felt like Claudia had forced me to look at my situation, then sent me stumbling into the strip lighting of the corridor. For the next few hours I felt worse. But the positive thoughts she had me repeat, sentences like, 'I am strong and capable, I am loveable,' stayed with me, they managed to ear worm into my brain. And though I didn't have a Paul on the road to Damascus moment, I think that's how these treatments move you forward, they slowly, gently rebuild your self-esteem. It's not one miracle, it's a bunch of things that work together.

I did return from Viva Mayr a bit stronger. Mentally, anyway. More hopeful. Less self-critical. Though, if I'm honest, that might have been thanks to four days in the company of Nadine. For me, hanging out with girlfriends is the best morale booster there is.

I'd always been sceptical of therapies that were left field but in my new life, where nothing was normal, the stakes were higher and the situation more desperate, I was more prepared to experiment. I remember thinking Princess Di's visits to energy healers and colonic practitioners were the actions of a desperate woman. Well, here I was, a desperate woman. I tried reiki, acupuncture, craniosacral therapy and these days have more rose quartz than currently resides in the mines of South America.

Who knows if these therapies shift my energy or remove blockages or if it's just a placebo effect but I always leave feeling better. Maybe it's because I've invested in myself, maybe it's because these therapists want to help heal or maybe there is something in these centuries-old traditions. I'm convinced the cumulative effect has been helpful. I know I'm lucky in that I

110

get most of this stuff for free because I'm reviewing it, but my advice would be research something that resonates with you and try it. But make sure you are a right fit with the therapist. That you feel comfortable with them, that you believe in their integrity. When it comes to healing, it's all about how much they care.

If I had to identify one truly transformative treatment I had, it would be the one with Michelle Roques O'Neil. A pioneer in aromatherapy, she is also a healer – she adapts the treatments to what you need, cradling your head, massaging your body, doing reflexology on your feet. It moved me forward. It's hard to put my finger on why, but I think it's because I felt like I could create moments of self-care for myself by booking these appointments. Or perhaps it was about the feel-good oxytocin hormone released by Michelle's gentle touch. Whatever, it made me feel great.

But one thing I've found time and again is recovery isn't linear. You can dip back and propel forward at the same time.

Linear, *adjective*:
1. arranged in or extending along a straight or nearly straight line
2. able to be represented by a straight line on a graph

During the worst days of my break up, I heard some local gossip about a woman whose husband had also left her, claiming they'd 'grown apart'. I had her number thanks to the innumerable WhatsApp groups having school-age kids seems to drag you into. So I messaged her and she showed up at my house two hours later. The growing apart bit may have been true, but the back story, which hadn't been mentioned, was that her husband had had another relationship and spent six torturous months deciding whether or not to leave.

We sat, broken, at my kitchen table. We have been bonded ever since. And one of the things we remind ourselves of, regularly, is that tomorrow is another day. Some days you will feel OK. Some days you will feel beyond shit. And you just need to get through that hour, that afternoon, that evening and you will feel OK, or better, tomorrow. Remember this, because it's comforting to know: when you are at rock bottom, it won't last. The non-linear recovery from heartbreak can be frustrating, as it makes it hard to recognise our own progress, but you will be healing in ways that you can't yet see – even when you're crying on the bathroom floor.

In the beginning, the brain won't allow us to feel all the pain at once. It goes into shock to protect you. Just as a child learns their two times table but then forgets that they need to stop when they get to a sodding road, the brain can only allow so much in at once. So you progress on some stuff and regress on others.

Psychologist Fiona Murden tells me, 'The brain kicks into action to protect us during traumatic experience in order to allow us to keep going. To survive a trauma, our brain initially dampens the response of the emotional centres of the brain to stop us from developing what, for our ancient ancestors, would've been uncontrollable fear. Why? Because that would've immobilised us and made us more at risk of death.'

Sara Davison, who has helped thousands of people on their journey through heartbreak, agrees the recovery graph is never a straight line up. 'But we expect/ hope it to be, so the disappointment when we take a few steps back feels even bigger.'

We get stronger but then we can be triggered by an event or a memory which makes us sad or angry. It feels like we are going backwards but it's just the brain releasing negative emotions to help us feel stronger again, so we can move even further forward. I find it very reassuring to remember Sara's words when I think I've regressed emotionally. It. Is. Just. Temporary. We move up and down the loss cycle until we have the tools to power through and out the other side. It will always be a process of back and forth but you will get through this.

One way to keep moving forward is to start to focus your mind on creating a compelling future that you are excited to live. It shifts the focus from the current pain and suffering and gives you something to get excited about. What would your life look like if you could wave a magic wand? Go all out. Happiness? Health? Rewarding career, beautiful house, contented children, handsome, loving partner?

I would not allow myself to think about these things. Not even dream they could be possible because I couldn't bear the disappointment. It felt like tempting fate. But actually, as the Instagram legend Vex King says, 'A positive mind makes a positive life.' Dare to imagine, try to believe.

Sara tells me, 'Life will always throw you challenges and a break up is something nearly all of us will go through at some point. Focus on what you can control and on a future that you can work towards step by step.'

Fiona talks about the complexity of recovery because of the unique circumstances of each break up. It will involve a journey of highs and lows. It's not a requirement that everyone goes through certain stages (depression, anger, etc). For example, someone may be fine eighteen months after a break up and then bump into their ex and everything unravels as all the memories and feelings come flooding back. Someone else may be still living in a house that they once shared with their ex and the reminders are constant and unavoidable.

Fiona says, 'One of the most important factors in recovery is how resilient you are. Thankfully resilience is something that is within your control and is quite often dependent on the strength of your social support. It's really important to reach out to and connect with close friends on a constant basis.'

I know first-hand what sound advice this is. Depression makes it tempting to close the door and to retreat into our sadness but let your friends help you to build

114

your resilience in order to move on. I am an extrovert, and am always up for meeting mates but, for the first time in my life, I struggled to get myself to the pub/dinner/drinks. I very nearly cancelled a girls' weekend once because I just couldn't bear the thought of being alone with my thoughts on the car journey there. In the end, I was truthful about my off-the-scale anxiety and my friend Viv came to pick me up. My girlfriends got me through one of the worst weekends of my life.

Yoga and somatics teacher Nahid de Belgeonne contacted me on Instagram after seeing a post where I revealed my aversion to sitting with the pain. Founder of The Human Method, a unique combination of movements that reconnect the mind and body, she is one of those amazing multi hyphenate experts who blends all kinds of practices to incredible effect. I wish you could all see her but as there's only one of her and I imagine you are spread far and wide, I will try to communicate some of her wisdom here.

She is big into breathwork. Which is another of those words that make my eyes glaze over. But really it just means focusing on your breathing. Breathing, it transpires, isn't just something you do as a matter of course. You can consciously change it and reap considerable benefits. One terrible day, I was desperate for X to come home. I phoned a friend and was so upset I couldn't catch my breath, couldn't speak through the sobs. Breathe in for five and out for five, she said. And, even in that terrible moment, it gave me a bit of relief.

Nahid got me to take long slow breaths, expanding my stomach as I breathed in. Which felt a bit weird. But as soon as I focused on my breath, I stopped focusing on the fact I was surely, surely going to be bankrupt, the kids would be in therapy for the rest of their lives, I was destined to spend my life alone, dying a sad and lonely death. The end. Which was my usual internal soundtrack at that point. It was an unexpected relief to be freed of it, even for a short while. Breathwork may sound like something super woo woo, but it is a tool you can use anywhere, at any time, immediately. And it works. You don't need to believe in it to experience the benefits and it may help you in a moment when you feel like nothing will.

Nahid instructed me to gather an enormous amount of cushions and blankets, and asked me to get really comfortable lying on the floor. She said it's impossible to feel really stressed if we feel warm and cosseted. And that turns out to be true. Try it for yourself. Build a kind of nest of cushions and blankets and let yourself feel the sensation of being held and supported. It's easy to think this kind of simple exercise won't do much but I realised it is about slowing myself down, finding a way to rest – even just for a moment – when everything in my body was on constant high alert.

I also visited Fiona Lamb, a hypnotherapist. Again, I was sceptical because the only time I'd ever witnessed a hypnotist in action he was a balding, sweaty man in a cheap suit swinging a watch chain in the student union

116

bar. The rugby team were transformed into clucking chickens and made to lay an egg on stage. But Fiona is a hypnotherapist who looks like a young Elle Macpherson. I lay on a treatment bed and she asked me about my fears. I told her that I felt depleted, my self-esteem crushed. That I am not loveable. She relaxed me into a theta state (between conscious and subconscious), when the brain is apparently most receptive to new thoughts, and introduced new ways of thinking.

'I am loveable. I am enough. I have strength.'

In the moment, it was a new and slightly disconcerting experience but I genuinely found it to be helpful. Rather than being a wonky, off-the-wall therapy, it seems to have its basis in a sensible established approach, in reprogramming the brain to thinking positive, self-affirming thoughts and establishing new patterns of thinking. Much like the well-regarded cognitive behavioural therapy or CBT. I didn't try this but friends found it hugely helpful.

My friend Sam once told me a brilliant analogy about negative thought patterns: 'When you are trying to create positive thinking it's like mowing an overgrown lawn – really hard going at first, but once the path is mown it becomes easier each time.' So persist with the positive affirmations even if you find them intolerably cheesy at first. Get your brain off the treadmill of negative thoughts that can take you in a downward spiral.

A few things that really helped me at this stage:

- Stop telling your sad story over and over. This is a piece of advice from Sara. Some people are super private and never tell their story. Some, like me, tell everyone. But when the time came to tell a wider group of people, there were some who just wanted the juicy details. As a relentlessly honest person, I felt disingenuous giving them the sanitised version but by exposing yourself over and again you keep the wound raw.
- Don't overload your friends. You need to realise that, however much they love you, there is a limit to how many times they can hear about how your ex is definitely, maybe, 100 per cent seeing someone else. So I suggest spreading the load. Don't call the same person all the time. And visit a counsellor. They are paid to listen to this shit.
- Learn to self-soothe. A word about self-soothing. I first heard this term from a terrifying baby expert called Gina Ford. She thought it was ridiculous that people (OK, me) could only get their kids to sleep if their heads were stroked till they nodded off. You then had to commando crawl out of said babies' rooms so as not to wake them. Gina was all about babies learning their own self-soothing. I found this hard to enforce on my infants and I find it hard to enforce this on myself. But I know I need to stop calling

everyone as soon as something dramatic happens. I know I need to ask myself for answers before I look to someone else. I know I need to get stronger.

- Make your home cosy and warm. Nahid has made me realise it's much harder to get stressed when you are physically comfortable. Get the cosy blanket out of the drawer. Light the fire. Buy some fluffy slippers. Light the sodding candle that's still got the dust film on top. You think these little things are frivolous but they are a sign that you are being kind to yourself. And you need kindness right now.

- Open yourself up to others' kindness. Taking strength from their love and support makes you feel less alone.

- Yes, you have lost the love of your romantic partner but you have the love of mothers, brothers, sisters, cousins, friends, neighbours.

- Because I was open about my heartbreak, friends left meals in the porch. (I now have Le Creuset guilt as there are a gazillion unclaimed dishes.) Friends also had my kids for tea and for sleepovers so I could meet with lawyers. We had plentiful invites for weekends away/holidays when, I imagine, I was about as much fun as a dry white wine hangover.

TELL PEOPLE YOU NEED HELP

Two days after X left, I got a call from my editor. She told me I had lost my main freelance gig. My one reliable source of income. It was a crushing blow. I had left my spiritual home of *Red* magazine a year earlier because the money was better and more guaranteed at a new magazine.

I felt so unutterably shit.

I messaged my *Red* editor, Sarah. I was worried she was cross with me for jumping ship for more cash. I asked to see her, and she agreed. So I dragged my emaciated frame to London, sat in front of her and told her everything. She responded with kindness and warmth and not inconsiderable horror at my predicament. She was gracious and generous and offered to help me. And welcomed me back to the magazine I love.

Obviously there's being vulnerable and there's being a hot mess. You want to avoid being the latter with people you don't trust to respond with kindness and empathy. But this was a defining moment for me. It showed me that you have to tell people how you feel and what you need if they are going to be able to help you.

Brené Brown, author, professor and professional sage says, 'Vulnerability is our most accurate measurement of courage.' For me, honestly, being vulnerable requires no courage. I'm almost entirely missing a sense of pride (which my editor says is a gift in terms of book writing) so I find it embarrassingly easy to bare my soul. In fact, it's almost a compulsion. I mean, I have revealed in print that I once pulled on a pair of jeans in the morning, wore them to a meeting and noticed, at one particularly boring moment, that yesterday's knickers had worked themselves out of the left leg and were on the floor.

The piece that I had written about my break up for *Red* was about to hit the shelves. The penning of it had helped me find my own narrative after the gaslighting and the self-questioning. It meant I took time to consider how I was feeling, why I was feeling that way, and what was the true source of my pain.

And when the piece hit the shelves, it meant I suddenly received the support of thousands and thousands of people I didn't even know. Some of them had been through it and wanted to offer hope. Some had read the happy-family columns I had written pre-split and were in shock. Some were men wanting to know if I felt ready to date yet. Some, like Patricia, wanted to tell their own story.

Dear Rosie,

My friend forwarded me your article, which I found such a great, interesting, heartfelt read, and honestly a blessing that someone else felt the same feelings that I felt and still do sometimes. Plus brave, and I like being brave and strong.

I am forty-four years old, with three children, and had been with my husband from the age of twenty. I fell totally, almost obsessively in love with him straight away; he was my rock and anchor and we were inseparable.

121

We lived in a beautiful property, all three children in private school, several holidays a year. We had our trials, as every family has, but I thought nothing would break us, we had it all.

Until January 2018, when he told me he wasn't sure he was 'in love' with me any more. My heart exploded into a million pieces and shattered. I persisted, telling him it was a phase and that we would be fine, people fall in and out of love all the time in marriages, don't they?

The next few months were hell, my body was covered in eczema, I couldn't sleep, eat . . . I was functioning – doing the school runs, the fake happy, the dinner parties . . . but the reality was, I was broken. As the months went on, he changed, late nights at work, drinking too much, no interest in the children, and I was holding it all together. We talked, made love, cuddled and then the next day he would shut down again, we spun around in circles until that summer.

I got a message from a woman that I didn't know and, not to go into too much detail, it said that my husband and her had been sleeping together for a few months and he had finished it with her. The worst part of reading these messages was that part of me was relieved; I felt a weight lift off my shoulders, that I could now leave him. I had done months of being miserable, confused and feeling constantly sick.

I asked him to leave, he cried and shouted and said it was one big mistake. He knew that I couldn't forgive him and that is why he didn't tell me, although I had asked on several occasions whether he had cheated. He lied to me, he swore on our children's lives and looked me right in the eye and lied to me. My parents' history is cheating and I just

122

will not tolerate it. When the trust is gone, I knew I would be a nightmare to live with.

We then went through the challenge of telling the children. Heartbreaking. The guilt. Oh my god, the guilt was unbearable and still is at times. When I watch them pack their bags and go off every other weekend I sob behind closed doors. But I had lost two stone in weight from stress and realised that my mental health was more important, so I needed to move on.

Anyway, the divorce came through last winter, I moved out of the family house a year ago into rented accommodation with the children. My life has changed dramatically – no little luxuries of pub lunches, manicures and weekend breaks away. But the happiness I feel is unexplainable. I feel like I have found ME again. I'm working, albeit fitting the hours around the children as I have them 80 per cent of the time, but I'm making my own money now.

My new attitude is to smile . . . a lot, be grateful for my babies and to enjoy what is coming round the corner, get out of my comfort zone and not to overthink or to try and predict (hard for me) but to really live and love life.

There is so much more to this but I refuse to slag him off, as I want to hold my head up high and know that I have behaved in the correct manner to a man who let me down in every way possible, and still sometimes does, as far as the children are concerned. What is sad is, he has moved on, he has a lovely girlfriend now, but he still says that he will go to his grave with this agony on him of losing me. But I had

to put me first, maybe selfish but I knew it was the right thing to do
> *Love,*
> *Patricia*

HEARTWORK

Books to read:

Tiny Beautiful Things **by Cheryl Strayed**
Advice on love and life from someone who has been there. As well as writing *Wild*, Cheryl Strayed was an internet agony aunt. She answers questions from the heartbroken with warmth, wisdom and wit. She is honest, insightful and seriously funny. Her take on relationships will give you good guidance.

Poems for a World Gone to Sh*t **by various poets**
Poems might seem a bit heavy going right now but the ones in this book don't require a degree in English Lit. They do remind us heartbreak is a well-trodden path and give you hope, comfort and inspiration in equal measure. It's split into sections: 'What the F★★★?', 'Get Me the F★★★ Out of Here', 'Keep Your Sh★★ Together', 'Let's Do Something about This Sh★★' and 'Life Is Still F★★king Beautiful'. The book also looks reeeally pretty.

CHAPTER SIX

Detach
(severance pays)

'Let him go'

One of the greatest pains of a break up is that this person, whose world was once so intertwined with yours, is now going about their life totally separately. There are casual acquaintances that know more about the ins and outs of their existence than you do.

There is a particular pain in being told something new about your former partner by someone who you hardly know. Someone who perhaps unwittingly reveals, for the first time, that your ex is going on holiday with their new partner or that they are househunting together or any other revelation that demonstrates your ex is moving on with their life without you. If you are feeling really shit you will resort to begging said acquaintances for pathetic crumbs of detail. What did he look like? *(N.B.*

The only acceptable answer here is, 'Your ex looks like shit.')
Maybe the desire for every possible detail is about control.
Maybe it's about loneliness or shock. Is it because you
still love them? Is it because you now hate them?

Whatever – it's over.

Five months in, I was at a restaurant with my dad,
talking through, in excruciating detail, the drama of
previous weeks. The hurt, the atrocious behaviour,
the unforgivable cruelty. Before we'd even ordered
drinks, I'd tucked into analysing X's emails, dissecting
his responses, surmising who he was with and what
he was doing. I was googling. And showing my father
screenshots of WhatsApp threads.

He looked pained, verbally lassoed the waiter and
ordered wine. 'Rose,' he said, while necking a glass of
red with undisguised desperation, 'you need to detach.'

We were in Bills. Tears were already filling my eyes.
The waitress handed me a napkin and a drink with a
kindly look.

An aside: don't you think it's funny (funny pecu-
liar, not funny ha ha) that every restaurant, every
meeting, every movie, every song, every experience
feels heightened emotionally right now? That your
senses and your feelings are dialled up to the max
on everything. Bills, for instance, has been the in-
cidental backdrop to so many occasions. Meet the

126

girls, take the kids, have a work meeting – but beyond there being a particularly good Aperol spritz, the surroundings previously barely registered. As I spoke to my dad, it felt like I was seeing everything through a director's viewfinder. The napkins, the lurid wallpaper in the loos, the waitress's tattoo. The music felt like a cinematic score.

Detach??

The suggestion felt like utter insanity. Even though thinking of X was painful, it was impossible not to. I felt compelled to obsess over his every move, even though I knew it was torturing me. Pretty much every one of my thoughts was me thinking about his thoughts. Ironically, I realise now that I thought of X after our break up much more than I ever had when we were together. I wanted to make him see how destructive, see how despicable he was being. I wanted him to SEE me. I needed him to see my pain.

My dad tried to tell me, as gently as possible, that while I was spending every waking hour thinking about X and, come to think of it, every sleeping hour too, X's mind was probably filled with someone else.

'Let him go,' he said.

What, like X was a beautiful stag caught in a snare? Tangled in the trappings of domesticity? Should he be allowed to roam free and rut according to his whim?

127

Had I been keeping him from a life of happiness where he could work and play and never have to do a sodding Ocado order? My heart bleeds.

I know my dad didn't mean this. He meant I needed to let go of the idea of X and me together forever.

Sometimes detachment is a long and slow process. The soaking off of a plaster. Not without pain. But gradual. A protracted demise that is occasionally intensely painful but often more a dull ache of discontent and unhappiness that erodes your self-worth and gnaws at your soul. And sometimes detachment is brutal and shocking.

For me it was the latter.

But for X? The truth is I think he was detaching for a long time.

Many of us find it hard to believe that our partners have checked out. Because we didn't realise. Had no idea.

I think of myself as pretty emotionally intelligent. Observant. I like to think I'm quick to pick up if my friend is slightly peeved that I've not been attentive or thoughtful enough. With X, I thought we were good. We were still cuddling, still holding hands, still having sex – but unbeknownst to me his heart was hardening. He was building up resentment, bordering on contempt.

How do they detach without you noticing?

If X was feeling unhappy, he didn't have the balls to say it. 'I tried to tell you,' he said. And that messes with my brain. Because I don't think he did. Or maybe I just wasn't listening. See? Who knows? Another lesson I have learnt the hard way, is how we can hear what we want to hear, how easily things can be misconstrued, how one person truly believes they have said one thing and the other person hears something totally different.

X didn't like confrontation. When I begged him to stay, when I said, 'Will we be OK?' he would say yes. But then he would change his mind later. Or his actions would say otherwise.

Some men I know were so worried they would be persuaded back into a relationship they did outlandish things. After deciding to end his marriage, one man immediately emailed his contact list to say that they were splitting up. That way it was a done deal, no going back.

My friend M gave me the other perspective. She checked out of her marriage ages ago. Slowly, slowly she fell out of love until the sight of her husband brushing his teeth made her skin crawl. But her husband didn't know. He didn't see it coming either. Or if he did he buried it deep.

But the truth is that even as I hoped for detachment (sort of), I knew that our lives would be forever inter-twined. The truth is lots of us are still attached to our exes. Financially, through our children, through our pets, through our Netflix and Spotify accounts. I am attached to X. Attached through two children who will always be the product of both of us. Attached through all the memories, the friends, the places we have been, the experiences. Our emails were linked. Our photos the same. Our names. Our house. All shared.

So how do you detach? First, let's look at attachment. You can't detach if you don't know how you were attached in the first place. Psychologists describe your romantic partner as an 'attachment figure'. Most likely your primary attachment figure. Why them? Because of the intimacy and interdependence that exists in your relationship. Your close friends and family can come a close second but generally they are runners up in the attachment order. Which is why we put so much store in romantic partners.

In a segue, you might be interested to know your first and formative attachment is to your closest parent. And your relationship with them might very well inform your subsequent relationships throughout your life. It's one of those things that comes up in therapy – another reason to go. I'm no psychologist but if you want to go deep into understanding why you might be scared of intimacy, or might be too quick to rush into relationships, then chances are it's linked to your childhood.

But how do you know if you are still attached to your ex? Aside from the fact you still think about them every fricking second? Well, I asked that question of Google (hey, I am a serious journalist) and come across a piece by Samantha Joel PhD who says if your former partner is still the first person you want

130

to call if something great or shit has happened then you remain attached.

This gave me a light-bulb moment. I realised that, though I liked the idea of calling X, even before we broke up I knew that if I had some big news, other members of #TeamGreen would make better noises, would have more time and patience, more empathy and more enthusiasm. So in many ways, what I was still attached to was the idea that he was there to call, rather than the actual calling of him.

As if to prove the point to myself, I called him when I lost my job at the magazine. Previously he just wouldn't really know what to say to make me feel better. Now he was cold. It hurt more than anything. If I had thought we were in any way still a team then this was a loudhailer moment that told me at a gazillion decibels that he didn't give a shit.

Who would you call with big news if something major happened right now? And how do you think they would react? I think it is worth working out who your go-to person (or people) is before anything happens, just so you know in advance where to turn in an emergency.

In her article, Samantha Joel suggests that part of the detaching process involves spending time with supportive people. People who you care about and who might step into the role of the primary attachment figure for a while. (Though maybe don't tell them they have been foisted into a role which they weren't even aware they were auditioning for. It might freak them out . . .) Spend the minimum amount of time with your ex. Don't call them to share news. Don't lean on them for support. Don't hang out with them. Why? It just muddies the waters. Time apart will help you move on emotionally.

If you don't have kids, then Greg Behrendt, the author of *It's Called a Break Up Because It's Broken*, suggests no contact for two whole months. However, if this person has been a daily constant in your life for years then this feels like sawing off your arm with a bread knife. I mean, they know everyone in your life. They know how you feel about injections and anchovies. Christ, they are the only person whose mobile number you know off by heart. Plus they, and they alone, know where the security key to open the sodding windows is.

But Greg has a point. Silence and distance give you clarity. If you are constantly messaging your ex, you'll spend all your time decoding their voice notes or words. The timbre of their voice. They could be wavering? Or regretful?

The truth is, it's over.

If you go cold turkey, you will realise that you don't need their support. That actually you can find that comfort elsewhere. And that seeking out their reassurance is unhealthy and unhelpful in your recovery. But for most of us with children, or jointly owned houses, or even pets, it's impossible to cease all contact.

So in this case, therapists advise walling yourself off to an ex-partner emotionally. That means giving as little of yourself as possible and expecting the bare minimum from them.

Since X packed his bags and walked down the path, apart from that call about the job, I made sure to give nothing of myself. If he said, 'How are you?', I'd say, 'Fine.' I ask no questions about his life. I answer none about mine. I am what divorce coach Sara Davison would call 'functionally friendly', i.e., polite but remote (*N.B. This does NOT come naturally to me*). And slowly, slowly I started caring less about what X thought and who he was with. This didn't happen overnight. Not even over weeks but over months. But by focusing on the stuff I could control – my health, the kids, my work, my friends – he left the forefront of my mind.

I hope the same happens to you. Travelling is a great way to get a sense of perspective. To find the you without them. Distance and space help you process. For me, escaping from the day-to-day came with freedom from domestic drudgery and distraction from the pain. Writers like Elizabeth Gilbert (*Eat, Pray, Love*) and Cheryl Strayed (*Wild*) travelled to make sense of their feelings – to grow and to heal. Travel helps you feel the sunshine on your face, literally and metaphorically. Plus it's empowering to know you can do it by yourself. Your first holiday will be hard. But healing.

When it came to holidays with the kids, I found it essential to be with friends or family. I wanted to avoid holidays where X's absence would be obvious – an empty seat at the table. The kids missing someone to grapple with in the pool. When the weather was cold and bleak, I booked tickets for me and the kids to visit my friend Tania in Abu Dhabi. I felt sick spending the money when finances were so uncertain but at the time I felt getting away was key to survival.

At the airport, we clung together, three fragile beings, encumbered by suitcases and heartbreak. (There's something about air travel that heightens emotions, isn't there? Maybe it's the transience, the uncertainty, the intensity of a new experience. I sob at any film on a plane. Especially dodgy rom coms, FFS.) But we arrived to the sunshine. The warmth of its rays and my friend's welcome were instantly reviving. When we returned a week later, we were still hurting but stronger.

I was lucky to have opportunities for more trips, which further fortified us. (And as a child of a single mother who grew up in Birmingham and went to a dog rough comprehensive, I don't take this in any way for granted.) There was a break to San Sebastian to see my dad and his partner, Ann, where I ran every day along La Concha beach promenade repeating 'I will be OK, I will be OK' with each step. In July, we went to Virginia to visit my cousin and his family. We kayaked down the Shenandoah river, trailing beer and snacks behind us in a dingy. We swung through the trees on zip lines at a place called River Riders. We went to the twilight polo. The children and I felt held by the love of my cousin's family. Slowly, slowly, with the help of family and friends, we were healing.

There's no doubt in my mind that travel, if you're lucky enough to be able to do it, helps you move on. Once you stop obsessing over them you can start thinking about what you want. What did you compromise on in the relationship? What beliefs have you suppressed? What dreams have you given up on? What parts of you have you hidden? What behaviours did you accept to maintain harmony? What behaviours of your own don't you like? And then you can think about who you are at your core. What do you need to be your best and happiest self? What do you want? What values do you want to live by?

It may not feel like it yet, but you are getting there – closer to your happier, better self.

OK, deep breath, we've tackled emotionally detaching but for those of us who are married, what about legally detaching?

The question of your legal position in the aftermath of a split is an intimidating and terrifying one for many of us but you need to face it.

For me, still caught up in the emotional pain, talk of finances and splitting assets was agonising in the extreme. But for X it was over. He wanted to sort the finances. He wanted to be free. So, looking back, I have to thank him for not forcing the pace legally, as he certainly would have wanted.

135

I know other women who have been desperate to get a clean break, or their exes have pushed hard to rush it through, but I think often you end up settling for less if you speed the process up. You don't know your value early on in the separation. You are overwhelmed by the idea of life without your partner. I waited and I'm glad I did.

Talk of child maintenance and dividing assets felt deeply wounding. Destabilising. A black hole of uncertainty. This was not what I wanted. This was not what I was promised. Yet I had to navigate it with grace and dignity and resolve. Sometimes it felt too much to bear. Then he told me what he was going to pay into the joint account. It was much less than he paid in before. The reduced amount felt symbolic of his withdrawing from family life.

I questioned the number. He responded angrily. He said he'd asked around and that's the fair amount. It seemed unfair to me that he could just arbitrarily decide how much he would contribute to household costs. He also said that he wanted to go to a mediator instead of a lawyer. Cheaper and quicker, he said, like we were talking about getting tyres replaced.

Faced with unpicking the framework of your life, what should you do?

I didn't want to contact a lawyer. I wanted to stick my head in the sand. But bills came through the door. The car's MOT needed to be done. And I kept getting helpful texts from the bank to say the joint account had gone into the red. And that was just the day-to-day financial admin.

These worries and fears cast dark shadows over my days. Thinking about my financial future made me physically shake. Do you have a pension? I don't have a pension. Will I have to work forever? All these thoughts ticker tape through your head.

My friends took charge. P nagged me till I booked an appointment at the Citizen's Advice Bureau and when I got a time slot, she came with me to make sure I went.

CAB is a life-changing organisation for many. The advice on their website is clear and easy to digest – even for the most scrambled of brains. Though I'd be lying if I said it's a cheery place for a visit. When we got there, the office was depressing. The rooms were shabby, the waiting room full of people who looked winded or jaded by life. There were boxes of leaflets on domestic violence, food banks, child support. But the woman we saw was kind and helpful. She talked to me about benefits you can claim and help you can get.

If you have been left high and dry these people can help you, and you may need all the help you can get. There is no judgment. No condescension. The woman also talked about mediation and lawyers and told me something I didn't know – most lawyers will offer a one-to-one first meeting free.

I was recommended a lawyer and I visited her in plush London offices. I decided I liked her and started to recount my story. Which of course made me cry. I realised that in no way did I feel ready to do this.

A couple of months later, I was recommended another lawyer. P came with me. We drove there in her Mini, her trying to distract me with school-gate chat while simultaneously getting me to eat something.

It's so useful to take a friend. Because they can help absorb all the information while you just cope with the fact you are in a lawyer's office talking about the dissolution of your marriage.

The lawyer was called Sarah Lambert and I really liked her. She's one of the best. Here's what I learnt from her: you will need the help of the professionals. You have options. Here are some of the important ones:

A mediator

A mediator should be impartial. They will facilitate discussion. They will do a one-to-one discussion with both of you before the session and so will pick up if there are any issues of bullying or control. They can't give legal advice but may suggest you seek it if necessary. It will be you, your ex and them in the room. And maybe some Bourbon biscuits. Your aim in the session is to create a memorandum of understanding and then you may need help from a solicitor to make this legally binding.

Plus points: Cheaper and quicker than a lawyer.

Negative points: If you are feeling vulnerable, they won't fight your corner.

Cost: Fees for mediators tend to vary according to where you live but the average cost is £140 an hour. Expect their help to be in the hundreds or low thousands as you will need multiple sessions.

Collaborative law

This is borrowed from America. You each take your lawyer into a room and try and bash out an agreement. (Remember the scenes from *Eat Pray Love*?) Your lawyer will have the opportunity to dispense advice and say useful things like, 'You might want to get his pension valued.' You aim to create a consent order which is legally binding.

Plus points: Cheaper that going to court.

Negative points: If you can't reach an agreement in the room, then you can't use that lawyer going forward. Plus you still have to sit in a room with your ex.

Family Arbitration

You both appoint a specialist barrister who acts as a judge. It's less costly than going to court, but still pretty expensive. When agreement is reached, your lawyers make it legally binding. Sometimes getting both parties to agree who to appoint is time consuming in itself.

Plus points: The court process is slow, and even slower post–Covid, and this way you get seen more quickly.

Negative points: Still expensive. How much it costs depends on how long you take to get to a decision.

Cost: A simple arbitration costs around £1,000 but it can easily be double that.

A lawyer

If you are feeling like you need someone to fight your corner, or fear that you might get ripped off or bullied, then find a good lawyer. It can take conflict away between you and your ex as you are not having to discuss financial matters between you. As Sarah says, 'You can make unpopular decisions and blame it on the lawyer. If your ex has lots of money or is capable of hiding money then a lawyer is useful in getting you the best deal.'

Plus points: You have someone experienced fighting your corner. You don't have to deal with the conflict yourself.

Negative: Expensive. Can be inflammatory if you get a bullish lawyer intent on escalating tension.

Cost: If you avoid court, then fees should be sub £10,000.

Going to court

I think everyone agrees that going to court is best avoided. Firstly, it is expensive. And stressful. And, as Sarah points out, the outcome is 'in the judge's hands and he or she might have had a good or bad day, which will influence how sympathetic they are to your case.' So lawyers and mediators will try to avoid you going to court because it is so expensive. When is it necessary to go to court? When someone is hiding money. Or just not at all reasonable or prepared to negotiate.

Cost: If you go to court the average cost is about £30,000 in total, but Sarah has seen cases of spending of £60,000–70,000 on each side.

You can find more information on legal issues in the resources section at the end of the book.

Here's what I learnt about the legal process:

1. There is a temptation to go for a lawyer who will pour petrol on the flames and be gratifyingly onside about taking the bastard to the cleaners. Sarah says the only people that attitude helps 'is the lawyers and their bank accounts'. Yes, you need someone assertive, but not antagonistic.
2. 'You have to have a rapport with your lawyer,' says Sarah. 'You don't need to be best friends by the end of it but you do need to feel comfortable with them.' I felt like Sarah had my back and it was about more than money to her.

3. This is from my cousin T (another lawyer): 'It's a game. He's going to come in low, you are going to bat it back. Try to think of it that way.'

4. 'Remember, from a legal perspective it is irrelevant who did what and who is at fault,' says Sarah. 'Lots of couples argue about the grounds for divorce and whose fault it is but all that does is take time and cost money.'

5. 'I always ask my client, if I had a magic wand, what would be the best outcome?' says Sarah. 'Men often want to keep their pension. Women might want the house. Then I always try and bring it back to the end game.'

6. 'Think about the children,' Sarah says. 'That's my line if things get heated. There will be graduations and christenings and you want to have an amicable relationship.'

7. 'Men will often come out well in mediation,' says Sarah. 'It's a bit of a generalisation but most men see it as a business deal and are better at compartmentalising it than women. And often they are more used to negotiation.'

With all of this talk of finances and assets and pensions and lawyers, it may feel easiest to stick your head in the sand. To push away the processes that scare you. But once you tackle the things that frighten you, you will feel better. You gain strength from knowledge and the fact you are moving forward. Look at it as if you were someone on the outside. 'I'm so impressed by [insert your own name]. She has dealt with this with strength, courage and grace.'

This letter from Carla helped me see nothing is black and white.

Hey Rosie,

I've followed your column and Insta page and can relate to your story in many ways. However, I noticed that there are no stories where us women have chosen to terminate our unhappy marriages.

It's coming up to a year since my life changed forever.

I'm a thirty-nine-year-old mother of two. I'd call myself an 'accidental mother', however, you can't claim that when you underwent IVF for both your babies, can you? But they were never my specific plan. I'd hoped to have children, but it was mainly the ultimatum I'd been given by my husband that prompted action. I was lucky though, how blessed to have them. They're at their dad's tonight and I have heart pangs that they aren't with me. I wanted 'me' time and now I miss them terribly when they aren't around.

I'd been unhappy for such a long time and felt for a long time that we wouldn't grow old together. But I wasn't sure how our story would unravel.

Our pact was he'd have the career and I'd sacrifice mine for the children. I found it hard at home, my identity gone, mother, wife. Where was the person I once was? I'd disappeared in the throes of washing, breastfeeding, trying to balance life and then being grateful when he got home from work.

143

But he'd come home miserable, constantly attached to his phone with work. Weekends were stressful, he didn't seem to take any enjoyment from spending time with us. He was so moody. And he drank, he wasn't a happy drunk.

I was on auto pilot, and when he told me he'd be away with work, I'd be relieved for the space it gave me to breathe. I'd constantly find excuses not to have sex and anyway, I had cystitis constantly. Something I now look back and wonder if it was all emotional as since we've split I've not had one incident.

I decided to go back to work, only part time. I was worried about our financial instability – since kids, we were constantly overdrawn. Plus, I got to the point that I think I was sinking and needed to have something else and find myself a bit. I was everything to everyone else, yet to me, I was lost. So I got a job. I enjoyed the space, I began to recognise myself. Scratch the surface and I could see glimmers of who I once was. I began to laugh again. Proper laughs, the ones that tickle you on the inside.

Would you say it was inevitable that I ultimately fell in love with someone else? Some of my closest friends have. Other close friends had seen the end of our relationship coming for some time and weren't surprised. When I realised I could love someone else, from afar, I'll add, I realised I couldn't continue to lie to myself any more. I couldn't go on.

We had an argument on Mother's Day last year and when he shouted that I didn't love him, I agreed. That horrible moment when you see the opportunity but you know

144

what comes out of your mouth next will destroy everything and all that is familiar. I did that. Me.

Even though it was my decision, the heartbreak is indescribable. Since then, I have continued to absorb all the guilt, his pain, our children's pain. I feel ultimately responsible. But I feel happier – much happier. I do feel a little scared about where I'll end up. We're currently working our way through a divorce and selling the family home to enable us both to move on.

I made the choice. For a better and more contented future. I don't know if I'll get that, I'm working towards it. I'm hopeful and committed.

Don't get me wrong, though, even though it was my decision the heartbreak is gut wrenching, the second guessing doesn't stop and the guilt, well, sometimes it runs over me like being caught in the rain. I feel upset for turning our children's world upside down. But I do believe that since that day they've had a happier mummy and they have a relationship with their daddy that he has to work at. I think now he sees that value in his children and the future they'll have now.

Sorry about such a long message! I just wanted to put an alternative perspective forward.

With love,

Carla

HEARTWORK

Books to read:

The Boy, The Mole, The Fox and The Horse by Charlie Macksey

A picture book for people aged eight to eighty, this contains ridiculously touching, poignant pictures and funny, clever, words that uplift and inspire. If you are too exhausted or fried to contemplate a 'proper book' this is perfect reading.

Rising Strong by Brené Brown

When you need encouragement to keep going, keep growing, keep getting up when you want to stay down – read this. Brown delivers hope, understanding, empathy and motivation. She gives you the courage you need to get to the heart of the situation. Plus she's Oprah approved. Enough said.

CHAPTER SEVEN

Acceptance
(finding you without them)

'We cannot direct the wind, but we can adjust the sails'
DOLLY PARTON

You don't want to accept that this is the end.

You don't want to accept the ownership of the blue jobs – those domestic duties that historically have gone to the guy of the house. The paying of the utility bills, the clearing of the gutter, the checking of the tyre pressures.

You don't want to accept that they can be happy without you.

If you are like me, you don't want to accept any apology that is forthcoming. Why? Because no apology is good enough, because you don't want them to feel the way they feel. You want them to love you. You want them to want to be with you. You want them to say it's all been a horrendous mistake.

There was a moment when X did apologise. But it didn't happen the way I wanted it to. I would have liked it to have been delivered on his knees, hands clasped in prayer, with a side order of self-flagellation and possibly involving heinous-looking medieval torture implements that did unmentionable things to testicles. It didn't deliver the satisfaction or the validation I craved.

I didn't want to accept the reasons he was giving for his wanting out because they didn't ring true to me. I didn't want to accept the lies, half lies or even the truth. Nope. Even though I knew this was happening I had days where I regressed and just couldn't conceive it was. Or days when I wanted to stick my fingers in my ears and refuse. I wanted to go on believing that this wasn't happening, that we had a shiny future of financial security and garden centres and double slankets.

But though some, or all, of the above might be true, if we believe 100 per cent the partner who has left is wrong, then that is a false narrative in itself, right? So why do we struggle to accept what they are telling us? Why can't we just say, he wants to move on? He doesn't love me any more? He wants someone or something else?

Years before my marriage imploded, I remember reading a magazine piece about a high-profile writer in which she talked about splitting up with her husband. She said, 'He just didn't love me enough and I deserved more.' I remember feeling so amazed that she would choose to reveal such a rejection, that she could be so pragmatic about something that is so injurious, so painful. Because our ego hates rejection, right?

I've since learnt the hard way that when we are rejected our protection mechanism kicks in. Just as we flinch when a champagne cork flies our way, our mind flexes to find a way to push away unpalatable truths. It's so much easier for us, and our friends and family, to think he is mad, he is bad or that he is, in all probability, on drugs. (Though admittedly this was pretty unlikely in X's case as I think the strongest pill he's popped in his lifetime is a Nurofen Plus.) The temptation is to think they cannot really mean it. They just want to get something out of their system. It's obviously a classic midlife crisis.

But what's a midlife crisis if it isn't a massive rejection of the life they are living now? Rejecting the slide into dad bod by working out, buying new clothes, adopting a new moral code, and the most clichéd of all – buying a penis-extension car.

In my struggle to accept what has happened, let alone move on from it, I came across the work of Byron Katie. She is all about taking the ego out of the situation. Our ego, not theirs. What does she mean by that? Well, imagine if you didn't have the defensiveness and the hurt. If you could look at it objectively like an outsider. If you could stop thinking about what's going on in the other person's head and think about how we make peace with what has happened.

Because, after all, we need to be thinking about us. Not them. Byron Katie is a counsellor and author and life-changing person who looks like the Hollywood version of a kindly grandmother. Beautiful, grey haired, twinkly eyed, Katie (it's a bit confusing – you call her Katie even though her first name is Byron) exudes warmth and, to paraphrase the late, great Roald Dahl, the goodness shines out of her like sunbeams. I'm guessing her house smells of fresh-cut sweet peas and Elnett hairspray.

She has a website where you can see, on video, how she transforms, in real-time, the lives of people stuck in negative thought patterns by gently challenging them with a series of questions about the truth of their situation. Katie had her own rock bottom, a spiral into depression, agoraphobia and suicidal thoughts, many years ago. She found liberation in her rock bottom and is even grateful it happened.

Imagine that? That this heartbreak could be something we are grateful for.

I arranged to Zoom with her and she spoke at length about how it's our thoughts that cause suffering rather than our reality. I agree with that. The suffering is in our heads. Yes, I may have got cold taking out the bins or wet when lugging the supermarket shop in from the car but it's the thought that he is not there to do those things rather than the reality of having to do them myself that is painful, not the bins or the supermarket bags themselves. And actually I spent too long in a state

150

of resentment in our relationship when X wasn't around to help with the kids or come to that party. Now I am free from that. I'm doing it on my own.

It's the idea of being lonely, the future projection of being in a depressingly overstuffed flat with ever-lengthening whiskers and only daytime TV for company that really kills me. Imagine if the only man in your life was Eamonn Holmes. (Shudders.)

Katie says, 'You can't be frightened if your mind stays in the present.'

I remind myself that, even in the depths of sadness, I am warm, dry and fed, with the love of family and friends.

Katie talks a lot about the ego and how it can be so negative in the healing process. This seems to fly in the face of all the advice that picking yourself up is about self-belief and self-esteem, but it doesn't really. You still need all those things. She's just saying what if you were happy enough with yourself to not need to prove yourself right to those around you, to not need to make them adhere to your point of view, to not need to win.

Ego, *noun:* Person's sense of self-esteem or self-importance.

The ego is about personal identity. Who we believe ourselves to be and how we protect that vision of ourselves. For example, I'm fun, smart, attractive, good at writing and hugging, yada yada. When someone rejects you, it slices through your self-belief like a Sabatier through butter. It rips your core identity right out and leaves it for the rats to gnaw on. In the scramble to try to heal, your ego makes some monstrously bad moves. The ego makes you want to prove your point.

Do you, like me, wrestle with wanting him to understand what he has done? How wrong he has been? Do you want him to SEE the damage he has caused? I wonder why I need this so much, but Katie helps me understand – it's because my ego wants it like a Labrador wants that chipolata. Insatiably.

This is why we develop 'truths' only we can see. He is crazy. Or a horrible person. Or has an oedipal obsession with his mother. If your friends' eyes glaze over when you recount your version of reality, chances are they don't want to be disloyal to you, their slightly deranged friend, but equally don't want to be complicit in your fantasy. They know, even if you don't yet, that the truth is he's just over you.

I think the ego must be why, if your friends meet up with your ex (which is the worst gut punch, right?) it makes you feel angry/vulnerable/scared because then it questions your story, you know the one that you were wrong and he's a bastard, and your story is the only thing keeping your very fragile sense of self together. And it feels disloyal and makes you think you cannot trust your friends with your feelings. In case they recount them to your ex.

152

Our story, that we are the victim of a terrible atrocity, 'Is the ego trying to protect its identity,' Katie said to me. 'It needs to say "I am the one being hurt".'

We try to avoid the pain of rejection because rejection of self is one of the most hideous feelings there is. If not the most hideous. It's the ego that means a child's anger at stubbing their toe is directed at the stupid pavement slab instead of at themselves for not noticing it was uneven. It's why, when you do something morally questionable, say queue jumping, your mind will scrabble for justification and you will find a reason to be angry with the person who tells you off.

Katie says, 'The ego identifies as you. But it is not you. The ego is nothing more than a thought system. The ego is fake news.'

On a dog walk recently, my friend M, who is one of the kindest, most honest people I know, said, 'I like to believe you are your spirit at your core. And that spirit is the person you were and are before you add the layers of fear and the consequent mental survival mechanisms you have constructed to keep it happy.'

At my core, I know I am good and kind and forgiving and optimistic. And a little chaotic and over-reaching. What are you at yours? Who are you without the anger and the catastrophising? Can you be content with who you are?

To move on from this, Katie recommended that I go to her website (see 'Resources' at the back of the book) and find the 'Judge Your Neighbour' worksheet and fill it in. But for a while I resisted doing this. Filling out questionnaires takes me back to doing personality quizzes in teen magazines. And I didn't ever get the result I wanted, so I used to have to fake my answers. But when I finally sat down and looked at it, I realised Katie's questionnaire is revelatory.

It asks various questions. The first is:

In this situation, who angers, confuses, hurts or disappoints you?

I put, 'I am hurt with X because he rejected me.'

She then asks, *Is the statement true?*

Well, on reflection maybe it's not. Or it's not as simple as that.

How do you react when you believe this thought?

I feel devastated, down, destroyed. All the ds.

Where would you be without this thought?

Free.

Katie told me in our Zoom that after I'd completed the questionnaire I was to go back to the heartbreak.

Try this. Recall a moment of intense pain and suffering. And think about how it makes you feel. You know, all those pleasant emotions like utter gut-wrenching sorrow, worthlessness. The drowning in despair. Thoughts like, 'He has ruined my life, it's not fair, I will never be happy again.' Then think about the images you have in your mind's eye – for me, this is X's face distorted with rage, or contempt, or disdain. Me curled up in a ball on the bathroom floor.

Katie wants you to see that these images are not 100 per cent accurate. That they are 'a movie'. The way you have chosen to remember them. But when you see these things, you believe the emotions that come up. She encouraged me to get into the here and now, to 'flip' things, looking for the opposite belief.

Take my first answer on that worksheet: 'I am hurt by X because he rejected me.'

Flipping it would become: 'I rejected X.'

Maybe that is true. Maybe I did reject some parts of him. Perhaps I did try to mould and shape him. I rejected the way he put his toenail clippings in his empty coffee cup that's fo' sho'.

What about . . .

I rejected me. I again lost a lot of who I was. Over years I cloaked so much of who I was and moulded myself into something more acceptable to X. I'm sure he did the same for me. And then, in the throes of the break up, I became someone I didn't recognise. So weak. So passive. I lost any fight.

Katie says to ground each turnaround in genuine specific examples, if possible three each. So for example 'he let me down' would become 'I let myself down'.

To find the truth, put the specifics of how you feel wronged on paper.

Katie's technique seems to come from the same school of thought as NLP, CBT and divorce coach Sara's 'flip it'. An attempt to reset the mind, to see things from a different perspective, a perspective that is more helpful for recovery and means you are more able to see difficult situations in a positive way.

So how about instead of pushing our uncomfortable emotions away, we look at them closely? And we feel them deeply? And instead of satisfying our ego with an instant reaction that exonerates us from blame and takes that hurt and transforms it into a more palatable anger, we think about why what has happened has happened. And how we can learn from it.

You have been rejected but that's a decision made by someone else. It does not change who you are at the core. You are the same person you were before this happened. What has happened has happened for a million different reasons. How the person who left you has been shaped by their childhood, by their work, by their life experiences. And the same for you. Their decision to leave does not make you a bad, sad, unlovable person. It's a reflection of what they want right now in their life. And what their ego craves.

Facing the truth, the reality, works in another way too. It takes away the power of the fear. In the same way once you have forced yourself to go to a spin class/talk to the alpha mum at the school gates, you know it's not really that scary.

'We fear the emotions, but we don't spend long enough in them,' explained Katie.

Katie says you have to do THE WORK. Yes, that phrase again. Which sounds exhausting and slightly nausea inducing but basically means looking at your reactions and emotions. The reasons why you feel the way you do. Katie said that this means waking up to the difference between what she calls 'the mind's play', i.e., the stories we have embellished and distorted but which now feel very real, and the here and now. That way you can free yourself from the fear.

So they don't love you?

So what?

You've got you. And so have all your mates. And family.

Katie talked about her relationship with her husband. 'If I think he's wrong we can talk about it but I don't have to prove to him he is wrong.'

Which is revelatory, right? I always felt I had to prove X wrong. When we are in a relationship and we disagree about something, why do we need them to know they are wrong? Why can't we be content with knowing our standpoint?

It's about self-belief. Something so many of us will have lost.

Acceptance is not about proving them wrong. Or mad. Or horrible. It's about knowing we are good people. It's about our relationship with ourself.

Six months after X moved out, I travelled to a spa in Spain with my oldest friend, Jen. (Let me clarify, she's not my oldest friend in years but the friend I have known for decades, since Brownies. Which we were asked to leave because our dresses were too small and our attitudes too big.) SHA is a destination of the super wealthy, for whom health is the new wealth.

157

Imagine lots of CEOs with towelling robes that don't quite meet in the middle, now on a diet that's heavy on alfalfa sprouts and light on calories. Jen says it has a 'Dignitas' vibe.

While we are there, sniggering at it all and at ourselves, it strikes me that my friendship with Jen is my longest and most successful love affair. It's weathered decades, times when our lives have diverged and times when they have come together, weaving out and then converging like DNA strands. Times when both of us have been caught up in our own worlds, times when we have been selfish or needy or a bit full of ourselves. But there is endless empathy, a deep well of respect and a joy in each other and a long, long history that means our bond is unbreakable.

What is it that we are really looking for in our relationships? We want to find acceptance. To find peace. And we may find it with those who are already close to us, our friends, our family, ourselves.

Katie said she has met so many people who have spent years refusing to accept their break up. And it's a life half lived. If you don't do the work (i.e. dig deep and look at yourself) then, 'the best you can hope for is that sooner or later you'll get over it,' she said. 'But then on your death bed your last words will still be, "It's all his fault".'

We all know that person, that person who is still angry and bitter. Who hasn't moved on and is still trying to punish the other person. I don't want this for myself. Do you?

158

So pursue your own happiness. Don't stay fixated on their behaviour. This is the route to peace.

However, while it's one thing to accept they may have had their reasons for ending the relationship, it's another thing to accept our new financial situation. Now we have tackled the legal situation, we need to look at money.

If your ex has made the decision to leave, it will affect your income, your lifestyle, your kids' lifestyle. It feels so unfair.

I decided to do the sensible thing. Stick my head firmly in the sand.

In the end, my friend Viv frogmarched me to meet her financial advisor. I didn't want to meet her because a) I thought financial advisors were for rich people and I have zero savings (except for a post office account with a grand total of £28.90 in it). And b) I always worry they are going to rip you off (of my aforementioned £28.90, hardly worth it).

I met Lisa Conway-Hughes in the bowels of the super-chic hotel The Ned, which was full of bankers having eggs Benedict for a post-trade brunch. She's a blonde with an appealing mix of sass and warmth. She's written a book called *Money Lessons* and she wanted me, and you, to know financial advice is not about stashing away millions in a Swiss bank account but about being savvy with what you have to live your best life.

159

She has empathy for women whose financial situation has been torpedoed by a split. She also told me some shocking statistics about pensions – women have, on average, a fifth of the pension savings that men do. I wonder if that is because, however feminist we are, however loud we sing along to Destiny's Child's 'Independent Women', a lot of us still think, deep down, we will be looked after by a man.

Lisa had some great advice:

1. If you find it upsetting to look at your finances, recruit a friend to sit there and go through them with you.
2. Work out what you need to keep you going in the short term. What savings do you have access to? Can you borrow money from friends and family?
3. If you have debts, keep a document of what you owe and to whom.
4. Remember, legally you are not allowed to look at your partner's finances without their permission so steer clear of their personal accounts even if you know the passwords.
5. Some women have a tendency to seek emotional help from their financial advisor and financial help from their solicitor. This is not cost effective. A therapist or divorce coach is a good idea as they generally cost less per hour and can help you get your head in the right place to look at money matters with more clarity. The financial and legal element of a divorce are factual.

6. If you are in crisis, Christians Against Poverty offer help to people (not just Christians) who are in financial difficulty.
7. Check your financial advisor is FCA registered and is 'independent' rather than 'tied'. That means they look for the best deals for you across the market.
8. Try and keep an open mind about financial arrangements. Women often want to keep the house but sometimes it makes more sense not to.

Lisa says in an ideal world you would have the financial conversation directly with your ex. But we all know that is sometimes not possible.

When it comes to separating your entangled finances, you want to be strong enough so you're not taken advantage of but not so stubborn you can't see what to compromise on. Lisa thinks it's important to get moving on finances ASAP after your split, not least if you have any reason to think that your ex might not be straight with you about your shared assets. But personally, and this is just my situation, I'm glad I waited a little longer as I just didn't feel strong enough to tackle it sooner.

Accepting it's over.

Accepting your role.

Accepting your financial situation.

Sometimes it takes time for the sting to fade, for the heat to die down.

And for the new to become normal.

Dear Rosie,

My first marriage collapsed in a shitstorm and I had a baby and a four year old. Just saying, it's fucking grim but it just might turn out to be the best thing that ever happens. I'm happier now than I ever thought I could be (while being still very realistically re-married with all ensuing bickering, etc.).

I was with my ex from my teens to thirty-six. We had a few rocky years after it ended but he is now godfather to my youngest child. I couldn't bear the thought of losing my best friend. But if you rip up the rule book anything is possible with a bit of space and distance. I even love his new wife. Obviously there was therapy and some painful, cold, hard truths to be accepted.

I was furious for a couple of years. It helped me massively when my ex said he was sorry and had been a crap husband and took it on the chin. I definitely had to work through all the stages of grief. It's been seven years and I'd say I only really let it go four years ago after I accepted my own shortcomings in the relationship. I didn't really want to accept my failures.

The truth is that I was spoilt and immature when we were together. I hadn't figured out that no one can make you happy and you can always choose how to react. I chose to react badly and really didn't pursue my own happiness and self-development. I think the fact we had been together since our late teens had allowed a certain immaturity in our relationship to fester and neither of us grew up.

He is a pretty out-of-the-box thinker and once he decided that he'd been a shit husband (won't argue there) he

162

went for being the best ex-husband instead. Once I realised I didn't have to hate him, we now have all the best bits with none of the shit. It's great.

Love,
Jade

HEARTWORK

Books to read:

Everything I Know About Love by Dolly Alderton.
Dolly is unflinchingly honest and her writing is often so truthful it makes you wince. She talks about how platonic love is central to her happiness. And the hideous, glorious, messy world of dating. It's about twenty-somethings and it can make anyone over thirty-five feel ancient, but this is easily countered by the delicious humour and sharp insight.

Everything Is Figureoutable by Marie Forleo
Overwhelm is one of the biggest emotions in a break up. This funny, straight-talking book makes everything seem more manageable. Truly. Empowering is an over-used word (especially by me) but this tome really is.

CHAPTER EIGHT

Growth
(happens on the edge of
your comfort zone)

'He's done you a big fucking favour'
AMANDA BYRAM

Life begins at the edge of your comfort zone. Apparently. Are you way outside yours at this point? Like, a galaxy away? Would you have quite liked to stay in it? It was cosy there, right? And you've spent decades building defensive walls, feathering your nest, attempting to immunise yourself against the vagaries of life by creating a safe haven, both literally and metaphorically.

But an atomic bomb has been thrown in and the comfort zone is well and truly nuked. And you are left a shadow of yourself. In fact, right now, comfort is as scarce as pubic hair in a strip joint. Your future is uncertain. You inhabit a world that feels untethered, precarious and gut-achingly unfamiliar. You feel vulnerable, exposed, raw.

And yet . . .

In the same way the waves wash over a sandcastle, there is something cleansing about the situation. Destructive, yes, but the damaged, the unstable, the unviable is swept away. You may not have asked for it but regardless, it makes everything clean and fresh.

At this stage of heartbreak, it's normal (if anything is normal) to experience conflicting emotions. Fear and excitement. Sorrow and relief. I know the positive is drowned out by the negative at first. But slowly the balance shifts. Perhaps you're feeling this too, by now.

There's a reason the most successful novels, songs and films are based on great change, dramatic emotions and life-altering moments. There's a reason everyone wants to hear about your life right now. And it's not just nosiness. It's envy. Because the flip side to this whole shitstorm is EXCITEMENT. Suddenly the world is full of possibility. You can choose to see a life of bankruptcy, loneliness and dying alone. Or one of infinite new exciting experiences. Kissing, travelling, new places, new faces, new opportunities. More sex, less petty squabbling.

Yes, you said goodbye to your long-term partner, but perhaps you also bid farewell to a future of elasticated waists and *Midsomer Murders* repeats. Maybe you escaped being the couple that gets to retirement and realises they have nothing in common. Or being the woman who has to send her husband the link to buy her a Christmas present when she has bought and wrapped forty sodding presents for all of his relatives. Fuck that shit, as my friend Kelly would say. This fresh start also offers a chance to grow. Which sounds wanky but is actually true.

'He's done you a big fucking favour,' said Amanda Byram, TV presenter, hot babe, fellow blasphemer, author of *The Switch* and unofficial counsellor to a gazillion mates. 'I am going to congratulate you on your split.'

I spat out my coffee.

What?! She was congratulating me on the worst thing that's ever happened to me? The most traumatic event I have experienced. Being kneecapped by rejection. Being sucker punched by grief.

'You get to do the soul searching. My sister has always been in the same relationship for pretty much her entire adult life. She'll never get the chance to explore who she is by herself.'

(Side note: maybe she's happy basking in the unconditional love of her husband . . .)

'You get to look at yourself and work out how to be the best version of yourself. Often this comes from a low moment.'

Amanda insists that heartbreak means you get to discover you don't need a partner to be happy, to survive, to function. And by this point on my break up journey, I could recognise that it took the worst of times to make me understand I was enough. I didn't need to come as a perfect package of two. That the saying you are no one till someone loves you is bullshit.

You can use this time to discover what's meaningful to you. What you like to do, watch and read. You can sleep through the whole night because no one is getting up to pee.

Unbeknownst to me, while I was married, I had been suppressing a whole part of me. I'd been compromising a lot of who I was to keep the peace. I wasn't forced to do this. I was complicit. I'm sure he was doing the same.

Amanda has some serious wisdom. She found herself on her fortieth birthday, newly single and a hot mess. I know, beautiful, successful Amanda Byram. The woman who sent men wild with desire on *Total Wipeout*. The woman with a career and fame, money and a fan base that fires out compliments like Trump does incendiary tweets. But . . . just before she turned forty, she had cancelled a wedding at the eleventh hour.

'My world fell to pieces,' she said. 'I'd planned it to perfection. I was with a guy who ticked all the boxes, but it felt wrong. I had to face that the fairytale wasn't going to happen.'

The aftermath saw her in LA, fighting an unhealthy obsession with thinness and slowly sinking into a bog of despair about the fact the husband and 2.4 children she had always imagined hadn't materialised.

'I crumbled,' she recalled. 'I realised I hadn't got it all nailed. I had a proper wobble. I spiralled downwards.'

She went on an odyssey of self-discovery. 'I needed to understand who I was, to strip it back. I read self-help books, saw a therapist, journaled, searched my soul, had honest conversations, did NLP (neuro linguistic programming).' It wasn't a quick process, she tells me. Think years rather than months. And it wasn't always easy to stare her own insecurities and failings down.

This is (some of) what she learnt:

1. Expectation is the ruination of joy. Shedding those expectations was such a massive game changer for me.
2. Honesty is essential. Even if it makes for uncomfortable conversations.
3. Being vulnerable is OK. Actually good. I used to think it was a weakness.
4. It's good to learn how to take a compliment. I used to be so bad at this. If someone said I look nice I'd say, 'Oh God no, I look fat or I look ugly.' Now I try to say thank you. The first few times I felt like a wanker but as we reject a positive comment with a degrading reply, we immediately imprint the negative spin into our own mind and also in that of the compliment-giver. I know people who, regardless of how they look, will always tell me they look horrible. And no matter how many times I try to express that they look great, they continue to insist that they are a complete 'mess'. So over time, I stopped telling them

they looked well, because it is exhausting trying to convince someone that they deserve a compliment.

5. What we tell ourselves is so important. Our personalities change depending on which voices we listen to the most and, in some cases, the voices can get so loud that we no longer hear what is happening in the outside world and disregard anything that might contradict or disprove what these voices are telling us. Just like limescale, negativity builds up easily and gets tougher to remove the longer you leave it.

One of the things Amanda and I share, or shared, is a fear of being on our own. It took her a long time but she said, 'I got to a stage where I was genuinely OK by myself. You can tell yourself you are single and lonely and afraid. Then of course you are going to project that. If you tell yourself you are a fun, fabulous independent woman then that's what you project and internalise. It's understanding you have control. You have the reins to how you feel.'

I reflect on this and I know it's true. When I can say to myself 'this will be okay', or 'I'm a special person deserving of respect and love', then that's what I get. If I do stuff for myself, go for a run, get my hair done, even wear a dress rather than workout gear, I feel so much better about myself. When I think about where I am now and how far I've come I know that life will work out.

Amanda tells me she gets her confidence up by 'saying positive things about myself out loud. I'm the funny girl talking to herself in the corner! I'll also write

things down. Things like "I'm strong and powerful".
When I'm going for jobs, I'll write messages like that
to myself on my script. And if I need my confidence
bolstering before I go for a big audition or meeting, I'll
watch my showreel. This is lots of your achievements
condensed into three minutes. Watching it makes me
think "You've got this".'

She suggests creating your own version of a showreel
– your greatest hits. For those of us that don't have a
TV career, perhaps this is a collection of photos that
you can skim through, or a list of great achievements or
compliments you've received. Then, in times when your
self-confidence is dipping, you can look at it on your
phone and remind yourself of how amazing you are.

Another good thing that can come out of a break
up is that, for some, it's a kick up the arse profession-
ally. Partly out of necessity, because you are now on
your own, you need to make money; you need to be
independent. But also because that part of who you
are is important in restoring your self-worth. Your role
doesn't have to be spurned wife/girlfriend – instead
it can be shit-hot career woman. And you now have
more time to devote to your work. No more time
spent watching that crime drama you weren't actually
that bothered about. You can use the thinking space
to really work out what motivates you.

Now is the time to discover what you are made of.

It's taken time, energy, tears, a lot of introspection and honesty with yourself to get to this point.

What can you do with your new understanding of self? With your empathy and your awareness? You can get creative. Get motivated. Do you want to be the person who rose like a phoenix from the flames or the person who sank like a sack of King Edwards?

Heartbreak has long fired creativity. Think of Ernest Hemingway's novel *A Farewell to Arms*, Amy Winehouse's *Back to Black* or Sam Smith thanking the lover who broke his heart and inspired his album *In the Lonely Hour*, saying, 'You won me four Grammys.'

So if heartbreak fuels artistry, does domesticity do the opposite? Do stability and happiness smother creative flames like a fire blanket? Can it be a coincidence that musicians struggle to find their muse when they are safely ensconced in a Home Counties mansion, immune to the exquisite pain of real life? Singer Florence Welch thinks so – she's been quoted as saying that contentment is a 'creativity killer'.

I thought that stability was what I needed in order to be creative. That early nights and solid foundations gave me the essential headspace to produce my best writing. I was wrong. Yes, the cottage in the countryside, the beautiful children and the strong, steady husband gave me the base from which to work – and I did so happily. I deliberately chose, deliberately created, a life that was the opposite of the one I grew up with.

And I loved that life. Most of the time.

But, creatively, heartbreak has empowered me. Propelled me forward. The last time I wrote with such

171

honesty and ease was when I was a student and then a young intern in London – when I felt rootless and unsure. When I didn't have the safety and security of the familiar. When life was exhilarating, but also frightening and I found myself living in unfamiliar postcodes. When I spent weekends on National Express coaches visiting old friends in their strange new cities. When we would spend our nights in clubs, abandoning ourselves to the music, then wake up in houses we didn't know. When there was no money to immunise us from the hardships of life. No chance of a cab in the rain or a hotel room if we ended up locked out. And I was the richer for it.

When I started writing, I realised my unconventional childhood had gifted me a rawness that connected with people. But in recent years, that rawness had been buffed away, polished smooth by the life I had so carefully created. Now it was as if I'd been dipped in paint stripper and my naked self was exposed. I've always had skin a few millimetres thinner than your average Joe. At this point, though, it seemed even more permeable to every emotion.

Successful recovery – from heartbreak, from grief, from anything big – is all about understanding yourself more. And part of this is understanding what has created your fears, what triggers you. This heartbreak can be a chance to address and understand stuff that happened way before your relationship broke down.

I know I told you that my mother and father separated when I was very young. And it took my counsellor to point out to me many of my behaviours and fears were linked to this. If friends came and went, or were more or less present, I was sanguine and accepting. But the idea of a boyfriend doing this freaked me out. I couldn't allow them that freedom because I was holding on so tight. They had to see my point of view, they had to be unconditionally in love. I used to test boyfriends' devotion. Make them cry. Make them beg.

The irony is that throughout my heartbreak, my father has been a big support. I feel his love in a way I never have before. It's one of the most positive things that has come from this whole thing.

Realising what is at the root of my behaviour is immense. Recognising that we are able to be rational about some emotional situations and not others is eye opening. I can see now that my self-worth did not depend on whether I got that job or if my friend called me back but it did hinge on a romantic partner being in thrall to me.

What is your self-worth dependent on?

Can you identify the positives from your break up, other than the end of a relationship that wasn't working?

Perhaps:

1. You get to discover you are OK by yourself.
2. You get to feel all the feels.
3. You come to understand yourself better.
4. You know if you can survive this you can survive anything.

5. You have been tested and now realise how strong you are.
6. You've learnt that it's OK to be vulnerable sometimes. To be open, honest and ask for help when you need it.

As mentioned earlier, my levels of pride are pretty low. I've written about how I found myself at rock bottom, a puddle of snot and tears, and I've written about my AWOL pelvic floor. So, for me, being vulnerable is relatively easy. But for those who are private, I know asking for help can feel exposing and even shameful. This is, or was, the case for my friend N, who has been through a devastating heartbreak.

Dear Rosie,

I was (still am) a private person, so this experience perhaps had a different shattering angle than for a person who is more extrovert. Not harder or easier, just different.

My privacy definitely increased with age and life experiences to an unhealthy level. I think I had reached a point where I felt utterly alone and that I had absolutely nobody I could talk to – even though I 'talked' to plenty of people day to day. I suppose there was an element of 'If I talk about it then it is real', but ultimately I just felt alone and ashamed. I felt like I was teetering on an edge of a cliff and that by not displaying vulnerability I could keep myself still and upright. I felt if I showed any vulnerability I'd fall.

I do find strength and comfort in talking now but only with particular people. I'm definitely honest and probably overly open with anyone having a similar experience.

This experience forced me to let down my guard and show my vulnerability. I've been touched with how everyone has reacted with kindness.

Love,

N

The judge-y comments I have had about my break up can be counted on one hand. Like N, my experience is mostly of kindness and people wanting to support me. But I have found sometimes that people look for reasons to attribute some blame to you. I think this is because – like illness or a horrible accident – they want to find a reason why it happened to you, even why you 'deserved' it. You must have done something to make your husband behave this way. Then they can comfort themselves they are not doing such a thing so it won't happen to them. It's their fear that makes them behave this way, rather than their judgement.

And sometimes people just can't step up when you need them to. There is something about your situation that triggers them. Or they are going through their own shit. Or they are just a good-time friend. All of that is OK. Don't waste your depleted reserves on worrying about it. Be grateful for the people who are there for you instead.

Growth means you can allow for all the different reactions you are going to encounter, because you are

175

secure and confident in who you are. And nothing can shake that.

And though I wouldn't wish for heartbreak, for myself or anyone, I feel that it means you get to look at yourself and your relationships with those around you in a way you never would have before. This journey will have taught you so much about the human spirit and made you an entirely different person. In a good way.

Life might not have gone to plan, and it might have given us a barrel load of hurt. But it's also given us a richness and depth. And this letter shows you how.

Dear Rosie,

As someone who's been through two marriages, and am now on my third, I thought I'd share my own experience on pain and growth. Two broken marriages by the age of thirty-eight, now that's a situation I never thought I'd find myself in when I was in my heady twenties planning my first wedding. But with time I've learnt to be really grateful for those marriages and the pain I went through when they broke down.

At the end of my second marriage, there were times of anger, upset, utter despair and disillusionment, regret for decisions taken and deep soul searching as to what I did wrong to mess things up so badly . . . twice! I don't think I fully processed my first marriage breakdown and my part in what went wrong there until my second marriage fell apart quite spectacularly. It was like my whole life had ground to an unbearable stop, my job felt wrong, my second husband was AWOL, partying

176

harder than ever, disappearing late into the night and coming back in the wee hours regularly with no explanation.

I hated my flat, and my circle of friends at the time all seemed happier and more cosy and coupled up than us. I remember calling my sister to tell her my second marriage was over, sobbing from the very base of my stomach. I felt sick, empty and everything in my life felt wrong and misplaced. I wasn't anywhere where I wanted to be with any aspect of my life. I guess that was me reaching the bottom. There was a LOT of crying until I ached – wishing for and wanting a different life. Having no clue where to go.

Looking back, that was a point I had to reach, to go through the pain to be able to build a life that made more sense, that was on my terms, and find an emotional place where I could be happy, where I could be me.

Although I was afraid at the start, I started having therapy, and, God, I soon realised how much I needed it. I learnt to express the pain and regret about my first marriage breaking down and most vitally acknowledge my part in what had gone wrong. And then address where I had got to in my second marriage. It took some time and it was very painful looking in the mirror and seeing what I was. For me personally, I needed to realise how I wasn't being myself and I wasn't living anywhere near the life that was attuned to me. My true self.

In both relationships, without consciously realising it, I had changed and the relationship hadn't survived the change. I had adopted a life and a persona that didn't fit with what I wanted. I wanted someone to love me for who

I truly was, not the image that I had projected falsely for so many years. It was a massive homecoming of the truth and it wasn't pretty. My therapist helped me realise that both relationships had, as he called it, 'gone beyond the threshold' – essentially gone beyond the point of being able to be saved. My ex-husbands will have had their reasons for why my relationships with them didn't work but I had my own stuff to work on.

I have since married someone I worked with, also divorced, someone who I'd known as a colleague for years. Ironically I used to give him dating advice when he went through his divorce! We'd shared our marriage woes over many a pre-meeting coffee and it was with him that I'd probably been my most honest. There was never any pretence, I was always myself with him, flaws and all. And in the end, his flaws have made me more attracted to him.

I have sometimes reflected that I wish I hadn't 'wasted' all those years on two broken relationships but have come to realise and appreciate that they made me who I now am. Perhaps my current marriage wouldn't be anywhere near as strong if I hadn't had the journey I'd already had. I had to grow and reduce my baggage before I moved on to a more successful relationship. So I'd say growth in my case was an incredibly painful but an essential ingredient to me being able to be happier and move on to something more honest and real and fundamentally long lasting.

I've now been married for fifteen years. I'm being myself as much as I can and I'm happy being me and I'm honest. It's an imperfect perfect relationship – flaws are on full display.

178

*It's not smooth sailing all the time but neither of us is plan-
ning on any more weddings just yet.*
    Love,
    Olivia

HEARTWORK

Books to read:

**Eat, Pray, Love: One Woman's Search for Everything by
Elizabeth Gilbert**
Read the book or watch the movie. Both are brilliant. It's
a true journey of self discovery, rich with humour, insight
and romance. I liked that it shows heartbreak from the
other point of view (i.e. from the dumper not the dumped).

***The Switch: The Secret to Overcoming the Pressures of Perfec-
tion and Finding Health and Happiness* by Amanda Byram**
For us midlifers, for whom our age seems a one-way
ticket to elasticated waistbands and TENA Lady pads,
this book offers hope that we can look and feel great.
It offers practical advice, with Amanda delivering on
the feel-good message of helping you find 'health and
happiness' through empathising and strategising. It's
not about break ups per se (though she does talk about
how her romantic life has been anything but easy) but is
a brilliant manual for getting your life on track.

How to check your tyre pressure

I've chosen tyre pressures. But it could be any job that often falls into a man's remit. These jobs can feel daunting and they are laced with anger and frustration that you are having to take them on. I confess I totally handed these things over to X, which left me feeling clueless and disempowered. But, in fact, most of them are not hard, and once you've done them you will feel so much better.

So . . .

1. Drive to garage. Have some loose change.
2. Park by air pump.
3. Open driver's door. In the door frame it will tell you what your tyre pressures should be for front and back wheels.
4. Plug the desired pressure into the machine and put in the money.
5. Unscrew cap on tyre valve.
6. Affix pump.
7. Wait until you hear the machine bleep.
8. Remove pump and put cap back on.
9. Repeat three more times.
10. Simples.
11. Now you feel good, right?

CHAPTER NINE

Dating
(legs or cleavage, not both)

'You're going to get glandular fever'

When my daughter's rabbits died she was devastated. We mourned Roxie and Cutie hard for a full twenty-four hours (I was not responsible for giving them names that made them sound like two ageing Vegas strippers). I made my daughter consoling hot chocolates and assisted in the assembling of lollipop crosses for their graves. But after the requisite grieving period, I realised she was holding back telling me something. Something that, even as a six year old, she somehow felt that she just couldn't say.

'Do you want to get a new pet?' I asked.

She looked at me, tears trapped in her long, black lashes.

'Yes please.'

We got some guinea pigs.

181

N.B. For anyone considering the acquisition of ro-
dents as household pets, they are by far the lowest
maintenance. You are welcome.

Now, I'm not comparing your ex, or mine, to a rodent.
They are neither so cute nor so easily replaced, although
you may at times wish to lock both in a cage at the
bottom of the garden. But I recognised something in
my daughter's grief over her rabbits that I had only just
begun to acknowledge in myself: even in the midst of
my grief and devastation, even as I was convinced I
would never love someone again, or have someone
love me, I craved the closeness of a romantic partner.
That intimacy, the hugs, the togetherness. And that,
like my daughter, I just knew I was going to feel a lot
better once I had a new bey. A new focus.

Love researcher Helen Fisher says searching out
romantic love is in the human condition. Anthropolo-
gists have never found a society that didn't have it. 'It's
a need, it's an urge, like hunger and thirst, it's almost
impossible to stamp out,' she says.

Still . . . you might not feel the urge quite yet.
You might find the idea of another partner daunting.
Or abhorrent. Guy Winch says this fear comes when
the brain tries to protect us from inflicting torture on
ourselves again: 'The mind tries to keep our pain fresh
and unforgettable by having thoughts and images of our

loss pop into our heads when we least expect them. It makes sure to flood us with anxiety and stress when we consider dating again.'

If you've had your heart pulped, a new relationship might be as appealing as a walk in the woods with a hangry wolf. And then there's the self-doubt. Will a broken heart mean you make bad decisions? Will your wrecked self-esteem make you needier? Are you damaged goods? How can you expose your body to a stranger again? A body shaped by age and possibly childbirth. Even more terrifying, how can you expose your heart again? A heart whose ventricles have been twisted and scarred by hurt and pain and betrayal. Who will want you? Who will love you? How will you find someone? Can you resurrect your flirting skills which have been mothballed since All Saints were rocking Maharishi combat trousers? How will the kids cope? How can you deal with the inevitable rejection? And just what are the expectations these days in terms of pubic hair?

All these thoughts swarm through my head. But still, I knew I didn't want to be alone.

After a piece I wrote appeared in the *Telegraph*, a photographer 'slid into' my Instagram DM's (how very millennial). He was a photo journalist who had travelled with Syrian refugees, documenting their journey to Europe. Which sounded interesting, and pretty sexy.

We met for dinner.

That's just a line right? Four words. But it doesn't convey the gamut of feelings it elicited in me. Frightening and exhilarating. I was heart-palpitatingly nervous. And questioning my reasons and sanity. I was forty-fucking-five and have never been on a date before.

Never ever.

I met my husband at university. Our courtship involved loitering around each other's rooms in our hall of residence on the pretext that we needed to borrow a highlighter. For decades I had kissed no one but him. Had sex with no one but him.

Back to the photographer.

He was great company. I was, to my surprise, enjoying it.

In the book *It's Just a Date*, by Greg Behrendt and Amiira Ruotola-Behrendt, which my friend N had given me, it says to not load a date with expectations of where things are going or what it all means, or whether this is going to be a long-term relationship or just a fling. Enjoy the date for what it is – a night out with a new person. It's a buzzkill to spend the evening analysing everything they are saying for hindrances to your future. Example? He has a cheese habit which will probably mean cholesterol problems almost certainly leading to a premature death which rules him out as a long-term prospect. If you spend your date interviewing someone or trying to second guess how they want you to be, it will be zero fun and, in all probability, unsuccessful. It's inevitable you will bring your own baggage to a date but be open, assume they are decent until they prove themselves otherwise. As my friend V says, don't meet trouble halfway.

I think many women, me included, are programmed to think that men are just after sex and it's our job to be the gatekeepers of our vaginas. Because we need to keep that carrot dangling so as to entice men into providing wedding rings and genetically superior offspring.

The photographer was cute. And interesting and interested. By 9 p.m. we were in the Groucho Club. Kissing.

And then I learnt that if there is one really, really great thing that comes from having your heart broken it is kissing someone new. Kissing is a delightful thing.

I don't know about you, but snogging was never really part of my marriage. By the time I'd walked down the aisle, kisses had become more chaste. I take full responsibility for this. I thought PDAs were embarrassing. They made me feel a bit, well, nauseous. I just didn't want to do it. I didn't feel that desire. I know lots of my friends felt the same. In fact, my friend S said that when her husband suggested sex she would say, 'OK, but no kissing.'

There's other good stuff about dating too, aside from the kissing. And what about the messages? The dopamine hit of WhatsApps, the voice notes, the SMS, the Insta comments? Post-date I exchanged flirty messages with the photographer. After so many months of angst and rejection, I enjoyed feeling desired and desire.

185

When X was extracting himself from our relationship, I remember the painful moment he refused to
kiss me on the lips. It made me feel so unutterably
awful. So rejected, so dejected. It was something I
had taken for granted, that intimacy, that symbol of
love and suddenly he turned his cheek. It felt like the
end of days.

And here was this new man, who couldn't keep his
hands off me. He was perfect practice because I knew
he wasn't a long-term option. He's a full ten years
younger than me. No kids. I didn't sleep with him
because I knew that would make me feel too exposed
and, despite all of the excitement, I had enough of a
self-preservation instinct to protect myself from further
pain. I also felt confident there was no way I was
going to break his heart. Because while he liked me,
he wasn't invested in any kind of future.

We went out once, twice and the third time on
his Harley.

I tried to remember Pippa Grange's advice to avoid
chasing the end game. She warns, 'We always seem to
be chasing a win – that's where all the energy goes.
Don't project forward. Just enjoy the now.'

The messages between me and the photographer
petered out and I didn't try to resurrect them. I knew
I'd be chasing something for the sake of it rather than
because I thought he was the love of my life.

Still, my friend N saw I was missing the dopamine
hit of his contact and she said we needed to sign me

up to a dating app before I lost confidence. T, my features editor at *Red*, had told me about Hinge.

Dating apps. Aren't they for losers? People who can't get a date by themselves? Who are such lost causes their mates won't fix them up? Even now there's a stigma. A friend of mine said her boyfriend, whom she met online, asked if they could say they were introduced through mutual friends.

But apart from social media, your only other options for finding love when you're older are blind dates and joining a cycling club or similar. And I'd like a snog, but not enough to pedal up a very steep hill in the rain. Or wear Lycra with bum padding.

Sara Davison, the divorce coach, agrees with T and N. She actively recommends signing up to a dating app as part of recovery.

Whoa, you might think. I've had more than enough of rejection, why would I sign up for the self-esteem shredder that is online dating?

Sara says that it's normal for your self-esteem to be low, especially if someone has left you, and especially if they have had an affair. She told me that when most of her clients say they aren't looking for love they are protecting themselves from the hurt they've just endured. But she says deep down they are craving intimacy and connection. 'It's our number one human need. If you don't like a dating app you can come off. I'm not asking you to go on an actual date with anyone. I'm just asking you to dip your toe in the water. Even if you don't find anyone attractive, it's just having that connection in a safe space.' She explained that using online dating wisely can help you focus on moving forward. But she has some advice to help you do this in a way that will support, rather than knock, your confidence.

1. Don't underestimate the confidence-boosting impact of getting likes online. Often it represents a complete shift from the disempowering and limiting thought process of 'nobody will ever love me again' to seeing evidence that people can and do like you in that way.
2. Don't just talk to one person online. That's a recipe for disaster. It's about limiting any pain. When you have five or six guys on the go, if one person ghosts you, it doesn't matter because you have the others.
3. Remember it's not about meeting Mr Right, it's about meeting Mr Right Now. It's about having some fun and not putting too much expectation on it. It's not about being back in another serious relationship straight away. It's about learning to love yourself again.

For me that feels right.

Signing up to Hinge would feel nerve-wracking and tragic alone but felt fun and adventurous with N, who offered to help write my profile with me. I had been unsure about which site to go for but a bit of research (aka googling and quizzing my friends) shows that there is a clear hierarchy of dating apps that you need to be aware of before you begin. There is no

point looking for long-term love on an app full of
swingers and vice versa.

Here's a brief rundown of dating websites as I understand them (analogy thanks to Mat Venn):

Inner Circle

Supermarket equivalent: Fortnums
Lots of CEOs and bankers and glamorous Europeans. I
was messaged by older guys and a deluge of sub thirties.

Hinge

Supermarket equivalent: Waitrose
A mix of guys, but I found there to be a tranche of
decent, good-looking, solvent males.

Raya

Supermarket equivalent: Whole Foods
The 'celebrity' dating app where everyone is preposter-
ously good looking and fairly pleased with themselves.
You have to pass a vetting process to be allowed in.

Bumble

Supermarket equivalent: Sainsbury's
The idea is women make the first move. Which is good

(no unwanted messages) and bad (feels like you are doing the chasing). Some men are of questionable quality.

Tinder

Supermarket equivalent: Tesco
The original hook-up app. If you want sex, call . . .

Plenty of Fish

Supermarket equivalent: Lidl
You have to really hunt out the good stuff, but there are plentiful options.

N and I went through Hinge swiping and liking. Within minutes the likes were coming in. And the messages. Which was good, and disconcerting. And there were lots of attractive guys. In hindsight, I think the algorithm throws you the good stuff first. So don't get blasé that there are thousands more where these guys come from. If you see someone you like, take action, because once you have dismissed them you likely won't see them again. And you don't want swiper's remorse.

Among the guys was M. He was six foot three. Lived near-ish and was good on the chat. He was obviously a recent joiner. His separation still fresh. He said he was an empath like me. He was single, attractive and seemingly available.

190

M and I went on a date. We had a great time. In real life he was handsome, funny and interesting. We messaged more than we met in real life because it was summer and I'd booked in so many breaks and jetted off on so many spa reviews that it would make Greta Thunberg's head spin.

M kissed me on our second date. He said it made him feel alive. Like there was hope. And that I was part of his recovery. It was life affirming. It gave me teenage thrills. I was feeling all the feels, just like all those experts had been telling me to. And not only was I defibrillating my own broken heart but our ardent saliva swapping was helping him too. It was like I was some kind of saintly saviour of the broken hearted.

In the meantime I was messaging with other guys. One, F, stood out too. I liked him. Clever. Fit. Driven. We went on a date. Drank pink champagne. This was better than loading and unloading the dishwasher.

We kissed.

'You are going to get glandular fever,' sniggered my friend V.

I decided that seeing more than one person is fine, not least because M had made it clear that he was not looking for a long-term relationship. I said, being a sophisticated woman of the world, that this was fine with me. But was it? And, when I properly thought about availability, I had to ask myself, was I available? Truly?

I think (sweeping generalisation) women buy into the whole fairytale thing so hard and think our happiness lies in being loved that we don't stop to think about how ready we are for the realities of a relationship.

What did I want from online dating? Truly?

Declarations of undying love and someone to move in and share my bed every night? Or a flirty fun time with nice dinners and kisses and holidays? It was almost like my ego craved the former, but reality was that I was only honestly capable of the latter.

Dolly Alderton, author of *Everything I Know About Love*, wisely says that men are like taxis. You have to get them when their light is on and they are ready to accept passengers. You can meet the perfect person at the wrong time — and that means they're not perfect for you. And perhaps the same is true for women, too. But rather than say, as men do, that we're not available for anything serious, we claim (because I think we really believe) we want long-term love while subconsciously pursuing the people who we know, deep down, will not give it to us.

Dolly's quote was a revelation to my newly-dating self, that men who had made it clear they weren't after something serious, really weren't after anything serious. I guess I had bought so heavily into the romance BS I believed if I was 'special' enough it would make any man override pragmatism.

I interviewed self-growth strategist Emily Wysock-Wright, who has some no-bullshit advice for women who have an unerring instinct for choosing men who always seem to leave women hanging. Her advice: 'It is

YOUR responsibility, and in your power, to close this loop by self-growth.' In other words, stop waiting for men to change and start the real work of understanding yourself and your subconscious patterns. Only through our own development and growth do we begin to break the patterns that are holding us back, in dating and in life.

Easier said than done, right? Emily offers three suggestions to help you change your story around unavailable partners.

1. We subconsciously draw in partners who we hope will heal our childhood wounds. However, they are usually someone similar to the person who originally wounded us when we were younger. Identify when this is happening in your life.
2. We have a hard drive of past experiences which contribute to our very being each day. Accepting where we come from, why we have values and who we truly are is the first step to understanding ourselves on a deeper level.
3. It's time to re-write some of the programmes you currently unconsciously run, by changing the relationship you have with your own story and your own self through forgiveness.

When we think about this kind of self-healing and self-development we can fall into the trap of thinking that we have to be somehow perfect and sorted and serene with unshakeable self-confidence before we dare to date again. But is anyone ever healed, is anyone 'fixed'? Do you have to be whole again to plunge into the world of WhatsApp ticks and navigating exclusivity?

Vex King, author, life-coach and king of Insta inspiration, believes you don't have to be fully healed, that waiting for this is just a perfection trap. He believes that real progress is about making 'better decisions in the midst of living'. That you can simultaneously heal the past while being open to the present.

In other words – what are you waiting for?

Instead of trying to heal everything about myself at once, I asked myself the question, does dating make me feel better or worse? I decided, on the whole, better.

According to Guy Winch, one variable has been found to predict healthier and quicker adjustment to heartbreak – finding a new partner. He says, 'It may feel wrong, but going on dates with a new person can boost our fragile self-esteem and remind us that there are many other fish in the sea.'

Malminder Gill says that when you are falling in love with another person you are in some way falling in love with yourself. You do your hair, you shave your legs, you are nicer to yourself. You are more inclined to show your best self. The other person appreciates that and so do you.

But I can't deny that there are downsides to dating.

There are the inevitable sucker punches to an already fragile ego and there are some less than savoury people that you will encounter online. Here are some things I wish I'd known about dating before I got out there and learnt the hard way.

A word about young men

It's a phenomenon known to internet dating, that young men pursue older women. My inbox is full of twenty-year-olds commenting on my 'hotness', enquiring with a sexual subtext as to my likes and dislikes. Some of them are fit as. I actually message one twenty-four-year-old back. 'Why not go for someone your own age?' I ask. 'I like women who know what they want. I like older women.'

Perhaps what they really mean is 'women who don't want babies or commitment'? Or who are confident sexually? Or who they think are easier to get into bed?

A word about the pen pals

There's a subsection of men that will message endlessly. Back and forth all day. You know their inside leg measurements, what their coffee order is and the intimate details of their childcare arrangements but they don't ever suggest a meet up. The experts disagree about whether you should just ask them out. Some guys just need longer to suss you out. But after a few weeks, I tell them I don't need another friend, so . . .

195

What to wear

Please feel free to ignore my advice here but I feel I am somewhat qualified to offer an opinion at least because I used to be Trinny and Susannah's assistant and twenty years of styling celebrities for glossy mags has given me an insight into what works clothing-wise. I mean, we all know it should be about what's on the inside that counts. But we all also know that is BS and, initially at least, there's a lot riding on the exterior. The truth is that if you know you look cool and confident, then you are going to feel cool and confident.

Plus, clothes are also an indicator of tribe, right? When I think back to my teenage days, what we wore was essential in determining a person's compatibility. Your clothes marked out if you were a raver, an indie kid, a mod, a townie, a preppie.

BUT having said that, the most attractive thing to wear is eau de confidence. And if you have that you can wear what the fuck you like.

I recommend:

- Clothes that are form fitting, but not so tight the lace on your knickers shows through.
- Height-appropriate footwear. I'm five foot ten and I think towering over someone only works for Sophie Dahl and Jamie Cullum, so I go for flats on a first date.

- Something that hints at good lingerie. But doesn't display it.
- Legs or cleavage, but not both.
- A bit of make-up. I don't think there is anyone who isn't made 10 per cent better-looking with a slick of mascara.
- Perfume. Subtle but lingering.
- Great underwear. Nobody needs to see it, but it makes you feel sexier, right?
- Moisturised skin. Guys go wild for soft skin. Just saying.

What not to wear

- Fake lashes. Well perhaps those super subtle corner ones. But that's it.
- Man repeller accessories. Turban headbands. Kooky sunglasses. Novelty phone cases. Unless you are going out with a real hipster in which case fill your (Gucci) boots.
- Anything too girly. Peter Pan collars, too much sparkle. I'm saying no to excess frills. And sequins. In essence, avoid anything Grayson Perry, unless you are actually Grayson Perry.
- Anything that needs constant adjusting. Adjusting is not sexy.
- I know leopard print is the new neutral. But it still freaks men out.

- Super booby is not good. Men can't help themselves and then it's awkward when they spend dinner looking at your chest.
- Midriff is best kept under wraps unless you are the age of Bella Hadid. Actually, scratch that, unless you are Bella Hadid.
- Bondage dresses smell of desperation.
- No heavily drawn on brows. The marker-pen look is not a winner.

A word about faking it

No, not orgasms (that's chapter eleven). I'm taking hair extensions, lash extensions, nails, tans . . .

Ovid, the Roman poet, said of painted faces, 'No man can say I love you, for you are not what he loves.' Another Roman, Martial, wrote, 'You are but a composition of lies. Two thirds of your person are locked up in boxes at night.' I think he might have seen my 'two sizes bigger' M&S bra.

I think one or two cheats are acceptable when it comes to your appearance. But no guy likes to think they are going to wake up in the morning with someone who looks immeasurably different to the girl in the bar the previous night. And you don't want to be worried that you are not good enough without your double Spanx/contoured cheekbones or sky-high platforms. Confidence in who you are is essential.

Know what YOU are looking for

We often have a tendency when dating to fixate on whether the person we are meeting likes us without asking ourselves the more important question: do we like them? I found it useful to have a list that reminded me of what my most important qualities are in a partner – it's much harder to ignore red flags when you've put your essentials down on paper, or in your phone's Notes app. These notes aren't meant to be a shopping list of physical attributes or bank balances – you could live without a partner with blue eyes but can you live with a man who has no sense of humour? I know I couldn't.

My list:

1. Kind
2. Honest
3. Able to give me a fireman's lift
4. Funny
5. Motivated
6. Fit
7. Has a chest with girth.

My friend N says you need someone grateful . . .
I'm still pondering on this.

New terms you need to know about before you enter the dating arena:

Exclusive. This is when you mutually decide you are not seeing anyone else. Sometimes there is a ceremonious deleting of dating apps.

Transitional relationship. This is the name counsellors often apply to the first significant relationship that comes after a long-term relationship or marriage. They are someone who helps you find your footing after a difficult break up. Similar to a rebound but more considered.

Bread crumbing. The activity of sending brief and sporadic messages, digital morsels such as short text messages, Facebook posts or Instagram likes, which indicate that you still like someone, when in reality you're unlikely to meet up with them ever again, let alone pursue a full-blown relationship with them.

Ghosting. Having someone who you believe cares about you, whether it be a friend or someone you are dating, disappear from contact without any explanation at all. No phone call or email, not even a text.

One and done. When you know that this meeting will be a one-time only date.

I don't want to give the impression that dating is all fun. You will need to gird your loins at times. There can be something soul destroying about swiping through these men, smiling hopefully from your phone screen. Or the small talk, which can get boringly competitive

200

at times. 'What do you do for fun?' Kill me now.

You may encounter men who are into 'cuckolding' relationships (when men enjoy watching their partner having sex with someone else), the demisexual guys (me neither), the ones who take selfies in their bathrooms with their tops off (they are always the ones who really shouldn't take their tops off), the ones who ask how high your sex drive is, whose pictures always seem to be at an 'up nostril' angle. Then there are the ones who reveal 'I'm actually not single, hence why my profile says ethical non-monogamy'. Yes, really. The ones who 'have a partner but would like to meet another'. Guys who don't take their sunglasses off for a whole date.

There's also the chance you will see your ex on there. Or your friend's exes. Which is weird. Especially when they 'like' you.

I have had a few disasters. But I have also been lucky, 90 per cent of my dates have been good. Great even. Work with a positivity mindset – go for it.

A word on who pays

I don't know any guy who loves it if a woman assumes he will pay. I know this is divisive but isn't it weird to expect them to? If they want to pay for dinner (and I admit that does feel nice) then I will try and pay for drinks. Or the cab. Or something.

A word on rebounders

If you want to know the signs of someone who is not ready for a relationship, these are the classics (also, really be honest here, are you displaying these yourself?):

1. If they are angry at previous partner. Neutrality is a sign they are over it. Anger, not so much.
2. Moving too fast or too slow. One guy invited me to his Majorcan villa without having met me. Weird, right?
3. Your dates are all about sex. Or extremely casual.
4. They care more about what their ex is doing than what you are doing together. They spend time complaining to you about their ex's behaviour.
5. You are not progressing through the milestones of a relationship, such as talking about them on social media or meeting family.
6. It freaks them out to make future plans. OR they are picking out wedding china on date two.

M and I messaged back and forth. Kissing. Messaging. Flirting. Ditto F.

M suggested we go for a run together. Thanks to my dodgy pelvic floor this involved nil by mouth for the preceding twelve-hour period.

At what stage does multiple dating become duplicitous? I guess this is personal but I don't think I could sleep with multiple people. And once you are mutually projecting into the future with someone then you probably need to make a call.

F messaged to say he needed to be alone to sort out his finances. It hurt. It wasn't devastating, but it did sting and it did dent my self-confidence. Were his reasons genuine? Maybe. Maybe not. That's the thing about online dating. They could have found someone else. They could have rekindled things with their ex. You'll never know.

M distracted me. We messaged and flirted, kissed and dated, went to the cinema. Went for walks. After four or five months it ran its course and we ended it, both grateful for what it had given us.

Then, two days later F messaged me to say he had sorted his shit out and had been thinking about me. It felt serendipitous. F and I went out for six months of restaurants and holidays. We had fun. I called him my boyfriend. Which was weird. But nice.

But in many ways I was still a shadow of myself. I could tell he wanted me to be feistier. To be more myself. But I couldn't do that, I couldn't unearth that woman yet. It might sound odd, but I am more truthful, more real in my writing than I am in real life. Which I think is probably a headfuck for anyone in an intimate relationship with me. I can't be that vulnerable, can't be as honest in person as I am on the page. So the relationship ended. Not horribly, but it made me feel sad. And lonely.

I felt pretty shit.

Dating brings joy, and intimacy and casts a gloriously sunny glow on the rest of life. But also the very real possibility of getting hurt. Are you ready?

Dear Rosie,

My friend bought us tickets to hear you talk at the Red *magazine seminar at the beginning of November. She did so not only because she reads and loves your columns but because I've been through an almost identical situation to you.*

Listening to you was like listening to myself – I'm just a few months behind you. Thank you for being so honest – but with humour – I've found humour has been an amazing tool over the past year! Also for the honesty in your writing too, it really is such a comfort to know you're not the only one facing these new challenges.

Inspired by you, I joined Hinge after your talk. I'm having some lovely dates and having to relearn how to make an effort while working full time and raising two kids!

I saw a great quote today: 'I'm grateful that things didn't turn out as I once wanted them to.'

Love,

Kate

HEARTWORK

Books to read:

It's Just a Date: How to Get 'em, Read 'em and Rock 'em **by Greg Behrendt and Amiira Ruotola-Behrendt**
This is genius. Real-life stories and sage advice from this hilarious couple (they also wrote *It's Called a Breakup Because It's Broken* and he co-wrote *He's Just Not That into You*). It doesn't sugar-coat it and gives practical advice like 'don't be too keen'. And don't ever, ever talk about marriage on a first date. Even in a jokey way.

Sex and the City **by Candace Bushnell**
Old school I know, but this savagely funny insight into the New York dating scene is a distraction from the darkness. The hideousness of the men Carrie and co encounter makes your dinner with Dave, whose height was not as advertised (in fact nothing was as advertised), feel much less painful in comparison.

CHAPTER TEN

Being Single
('you need to take a man sabbatical')

'Being single and happy is a super power'

Does single = social reject, unworthy and less than? Will it mean dying alone in a flat full of old newspapers, mangy cats and congealed tubs of supermarket hummus?

Is singledom just a state of purgatory? Something to be endured until you find happiness with another? Or is there satisfaction to be found in the single state, if you accept it rather than pining after the fairytale? That happy-ever-after dream – the one with him the square-jawed prince and you with the tiny waist and the sodding tiara – has been packaged up and pumped into our consciousness since we saw our first Disney film.

My friend, author and love expert Natasha Lunn, points out that sometimes societal pressures make it

206

hard to distinguish what we are told we want from what we really want. 'It can be difficult to separate what you truly desire from what you've been taught to want, particularly when it comes to love,' she says. 'Do you want to get married because you see it as a chance to create a meaningful commitment or because you feel a societal pressure to? Do you want to have a baby because you long to be a mother or because you assume it's a box that has to be ticked in order to be happy? Sometimes, even when we think we are making these decisions from a true place, there are cultural expectations and assumptions and family histories pressed up against our thoughts which can make it tricky to figure out what we really desire for ourselves.'

Do we desire a romantic relationship or is it just drilled into us, like teeth brushing and wiping front to back, or because we REALLY WANT IT?

Erm . . . just checking.

Nope. I definitely do want romantic love. I know it will make me feel better. I try hard to unpick why. Is it that I want validation from someone else? Is it a need for closeness and connection? I look deep inside myself for the reasons and I come up with this, rather unhelpful answer: I. JUST. DO. Which I guess is interesting in itself. For me, a romantic partner feels like a primal need.

There's also no doubt that new romantic love can act as a plaster over the old wound, a barrier that keeps everything somewhat in place and the agony at bay. Nicky Clinch says, 'The greatest way to block out pain is to fall in love with someone else. Love is one of the biggest drugs there is. Love and sex. [In my marriage] I was constantly thinking I can find someone better and then after a while I realised wherever I go next I'm going to bring all this unhealed stuff with me and I'm probably going to end up in the same place.'

This makes me feel a little better about my uncoupled nature. I am not a single loser, no, I am a wise and reflective woman who is healing and learning.

Nicky warns about rushing into a new relationship too quickly, before you're ready, 'It always comes to bite you on the bottom. It never works and it never lasts.'

Understood. But I also still really wanted a boyfriend.

While I was trying to embrace the positives of my new single self, I went on a 'divorce retreat' run by Sara Davison, the Jimmy Choo-wearing life coach. There were twenty or so other broken-hearted individuals. It was pissing with rain and as I looked around at the motley crew of other love rejects I felt so, so sad. We were just humans longing for meaningful and profound bonding and, lacking it with our former partners, here we all were on a divorce retreat, looking to find it somewhere else.

When we were done dissecting our lives and loves at the end of the first day, we went for a curry together. All of us with the pain balled inside of us, all of us with smiles plastered on our faces. I felt like a fresher at university. Only considerably more jaded. Other visitors to that curry house – the family celebrating a sixteenth birthday, the men enjoying a madras post golf – they wouldn't guess the turmoil that existed within all of us.

When I woke on Sunday morning I was nursing a white wine hangover and biryani bloat. So I wasn't exactly feeling chipper when Sara asked us to write down our worst fears about love.

My number one was that no one would ever love me again. W, an optician in his fifties who had been left by his wife, tried his best to assure me that this would not be a reality, but I realised that I did believe it in my heart. The truth was, I didn't think I would feel fixed, whole, happy, until I found a partner again. And I didn't think anyone would ever want me.

When my relationship with F came to an end, even though its demise was mercifully brief, it sent me spiralling downwards into self-doubt. In the dying throes of the relationship, I spent the day at the beach with my kids and my friend Sam and her family. I was present physically, but mentally wrestling with a gut-gripping anxiety about whether I was now unpartnered and therefore unloved. My phone became my torturer again but I couldn't stay away from it. Like Gollum with the ring.

The kids deserved more from me.

I deserved more from me.

I remember a friend telling me that her mother, post-split from her father, had been far more interested in finding and pleasing a man than she was in parenting. Their relationship was irrevocably damaged by her behaviour. I was determined not to do this but I could also see how easy it was to fall into this trap. How desperate you might become for validation. How you might feel your happiness was dependent on a man loving you.

If I'm honest, I do feel that my happiness is increased by being in a romantic relationship. And that frustrates me. I have lots of amazing, funny friends who I know like me, I have the support of a brilliant family, and yet I do seek out romantic relationships. Why?

Psychologist Fiona Murden tells me I probably have high interpersonal needs, particularly affection. She talks about our needs for inclusion, control and affection – the things that motivate us.

Do you believe the people who say they are happy being single? I didn't. Yeah, right, I'd always think . . . Celebrities always say that and then show up, a few weeks later, looking all loved up, wearing eau de oxytocin, with a handsome partner on their arm. Like the ones who say they are happy being plus size, then slim down and confess it was all BS. Even Dolly Alderton, a walking advert for single life, who extols the joys of female friendships and star-fishing alone in bed, yoyos between saying her life is rich and full without a romantic relationship and saying how next-level shit being by yourself is.

However, some of the men I've dated have said, 'I'm happy being single.' Why would they say that if they weren't? But how? How do you get comfortable with being on your own? Or how do you come to terms with the idea that the relationship you are in might not be forever? No matter how much I try to understand that other people can be happy single, I cannot imagine that my own true happiness is possible outside of a relationship.

'How about you take a man sabbatical?' said my friend P.

I didn't want to take one. I really didn't want to take one.

Because (and these are not rational thoughts or ones I am particularly proud of) . . .

- If I leave the search for love I'll be older and less attractive when I go back to it.
- All the good ones will get taken if I'm not out there looking for them (scarcity mindset).
- I want love. And cuddles. Now, not later.
- And someone to say good night to.
- And someone to wake up with in the morning.

But when your desire for a partner comes from fear (of being alone, of being unloved, of being rejected), you can go for less than you deserve. When the search for love and connection is fear-based it's always about what you could lose and so you have to hold on tight,

be perfect. I reckon if you are not afraid of being on
your own then you are different in a relationship. You
are motivated not by fear but by genuine desire to be
with that person. You see them not as a life buoy you
can cling to but the salt on your chips, the orange peel
in your cocktail.

I knew I needed to make myself stronger. I could
see it without actually wanting to do it, which was a
headfuck. I understood what I needed, which was to
build my resilience. But how did I do that? How do
we make ourselves more resilient? I began to understand
that the way to deal with my innate terror of romantic
rejection was to make rejection less of an issue.

Elizabeth Day – beautiful, successful, smart Elizabeth
Day – talked me through how to deal with rejection.
Because yes, she has been rejected. Or actually, let's
reframe that, not rejection, but a relationship not
working out.

'Life has a frustrating habit of not accommodating
these visions [of walking off into the sunset],' she said
about the end of her own marriage and other relationships. 'Simply put: real people do not act according to
your script because they have their own stuff to deal
with. Realising this was a major breakthrough for me.
For the first time in my life, I had to learn that rejection
was not necessarily a personal indictment of who I was
but a result of the infinite nuance of what the other
person was going through, which in turn was the
consequence of an intricate chain of events, shaped by

212

their own experiences, and their own family dynamics and past relationships, that had literally nothing to do with me.'

Whoah. So someone could not want to be with you because of their shit, not because you are defective?

This may sound obvious to you but to me it was revelatory. I always thought if I was smart, sexy, funny enough then I could win over anyone. And that made me be the person I thought people wanted me to be. But if you are not your true self – which in my case is warm, loving, prone to hyperbole and slightly chaotic – then how can anyone love the true you?

Elizabeth then told me that she'd discovered the hard way that, 'It's more important to be real than perfect.'

This hit home. I twisted who I was to try to win back X, to try to save our family. And then I went straight from rock bottom to presenting myself as the perpetually shiny and fun online girlfriend-to-be who always guarantees you a good time and doesn't require anything from you except another cocktail please. I had lost sight of my authenticity in the effort to always please others. Because, while the shiny version of yourself may find love, in some way you lose faith that the real you, the non-shiny version is valuable. And loveable.

It's not surprising if you are questioning your own value and worthiness at this point in your split, because you feel your partner rejected you. Which hurts like hell (understatement). But have they truly rejected you? They have rejected how they feel in the relationship.

Not you *per se.* Their needs were not being met. But though this undoubtedly was about you to some extent, to a large part it will be more about where they are and how they have changed.

It's good to address the assumption – if on any level you have made one – that if you are not in a relationship your life is somehow on hold. On pause till the real stuff of hearts and flowers and cosy meals *a deux* happens.

Amanda Byram tells me she had a moment, on a boat off the coast of New Zealand, when she realised this is what she had been doing. 'I saw a big whale right beside the boat. Everyone went shhh. Then I saw the second whale. The first thing I thought? I'm so sad I don't get to share this with anyone. Then I had a second thought. It doesn't matter that I'm alone. I'm seeing this with my eyes. They'd be looking at it with their eyes. This is my moment.'

Reframe it. There is only shame in being alone if you see it that way.

Have you noticed that if you tell a story from a certain angle, people will agree and they will leave your interaction with that viewpoint imprinted in their mind? As will you. Be mindful of the story you are telling yourself and others about being single. Own the narrative and make it a positive one.

I'm wary of bullshitting though – because that is the road to ruin. No one's asking you to fake what you don't feel. But try hard to find the positives.

The truth is that a romantic partner often won't provide the validation we are looking for anyway. True, lasting validation comes from us. And, I think, from our girlfriends.

Lockdown was interesting in that lots of my friends reported a dip in confidence because they were relying solely on their romantic partners to give them compliments. And those compliments weren't exactly forthcoming in a time of 24/7 sweatpants, Zoom calls and a global pandemic. But the truth is, for a lot of us, it's your girlfriends who remember you have an important interview that day or a doctor's appointment. It's women who will notice you've had your hair cut or that your skin is looking extra glowy. Your girlfriends make you feel special. And if even your girlfriends can't quite fill the gap you feel at being single, maybe the solution to filling the emptiness is resilience and independence rather than pursuing another relationship.

'You must not see yourself as unlovable,' says my cousin E. Firmly.

'You are enough,' says Nicky Clinch. 'That's the core to all our healing, really. Sussing out that we don't need someone else to feel that worth. Maybe that's a mistake we make when we get into a marriage in the first place.'

She tells me that, when she split up from her husband, 'I was insecure and wounded. I needed to learn how to love myself, fulfil myself and nourish myself. Have my needs met without needing anyone else. That's

215

probably the greatest gift I got from my separation.'

I decided that I was determined to use this time alone to good effect. Determined to get to the stage where a relationship was a nice-to-have not a need-to-have. I do believe I've got to a point where I am much more balanced about it; where I can walk away if it's not making me happy. Perhaps it's because my self-confidence is rebuilding. Perhaps because I really try and absorb the love of my family and friends; really feel it.

Dr Jenny Taitz, clinical psychologist and author of *How to Be Single and Happy*, looks at being single as your chance to figure out your own personal 'mission statement'. She says this is the critical time to figure out who you are and what you stand for. 'When we're not in a relationship we really have some time to get clear about what matters to us and what we value,' she explains.

Know the world doesn't end if you don't have a partner. As I started to feel better and stronger I could focus on the children. And my friends and my family. I find myself in a space where I can give back to them.

My heartbreak had sucked me into a vortex where I could only really deal with my pain. I wasn't able to help others. Now I see a million things are happening in the lives of my friends and family. Life has thrown up some new curveballs for my nearest and dearest. And I can help. I can cook them dinner.

N.B. I'm a terrible cook. I can buy dinner then as-
semble it. Everyone is happier with that.

I've realised a romantic relationship takes up time. It
takes up brain space. It takes precedence over many
other thoughts, especially if it is going wrong. Actually,
even if it's going right. When will they call? What will
you wear? What did that last text mean? Do you fancy
them? Do they fancy you? But does the gap left by a
romantic partner feel like a lack? Does alone time make
you feel empty? Can you enjoy your own company?
For me that has always been an oxymoron.

But slowly that is changing. Immediately post-split,
any time spent solo made my mood plummet. My
mind was instantly consumed with negative thoughts.
But as I get stronger I am able to use time alone to
reflect and take stock. To think about where I am going
(metaphorically, not literally) and what I am doing.

It's tempting to see yourself as less worthy socially
if you are not in a romantic relationship. Will you
get invited to fewer things if you don't come as
a package? Will you find yourself sidelined from
dinner parties, shunned from picnics and days out? I
sincerely hope not. I mean, FFS, it's not the 1950s.
But some people are threatened by single people.
Remember Bridget Jones sarcastically explaining to
a dinner party of 'smug marrieds' that underneath

the clothes of single people, their whole bodies are covered in scales? My mother's generation experienced social exclusion from other women who thought they might make off with their husbands. Or that divorce might be catching.

Yet I don't experience any rejection. People invite us as a family of three, we invite them. What I do socially has shifted slightly – no couples' evenings, obviously – but that's OK. I'm grateful for this because being a social outcast is one of my biggest fears. I think my paranoia comes from a childhood where my mum and I were outsiders. Poor relations. But also I think that was down to it being the 1970s and my mum's anxiety and discomfort in social situations – some of which was down to the prejudice she encountered as a single woman.

I now believe you can heal in a relationship or out of one but the important thing is to be self-aware. To use this time to work out why you desire certain qualities in someone and fear others. It's also worth thinking about what makes you feel uncomfortable. In romantic relationships, yes, but in relationships full stop. Do you hate it when someone doesn't message you as much as you think they should? Or the opposite – perhaps you feel smothered by too much attention? It's worth reflecting on why certain behaviours press your buttons. The more you know yourself the less likely you are to freak out when one of those buttons is pressed.

218

Self-awareness doesn't mean that you don't feel anger or paranoia or rejection any more, of course. It just means that you have more of an understanding of why you feel this way. And it puts the responsibility for change on your own shoulders. People learn how to treat us from the way we treat ourselves. So use this time to treat yourself with the kindness, understanding and patience that you'd give to a friend who was taking her own first, tentative steps into a new single life. You wouldn't lay down the law to your friend about whether she should or shouldn't date, or whether she should or shouldn't stay single. You'd trust that she would make the right decision for herself at the right time. And if a period of singledom (however enforced and unwelcome) is about anything, it's about building this internal self-trust. Having faith that you know yourself well enough to make the right choices in future relationships. Self-trust means learning to recognise how you're feeling in the moment, how resilient you are, how vulnerable. Without judging it. The timing on new relationships is going to be different for everyone.

In reality, I still firmly believe that having a romantic partner does enhance my life. I love loving and being loved. And I recognise that about myself and own it. That's part of who I am. But it makes me really happy that, these days, my whole self-esteem doesn't hinge on being in a relationship. In a weird twist (and we are used to these now, right?) it's taken being rejected to know that to be true about myself.

'The irony is, once you are happy with yourself you will meet someone,' says Amanda Byram. 'I got to the point when I was genuinely OK by myself and within three days I met my husband.'

It's not luck, people.

Dear Rosie,

I literally threw myself into dating anyone to get over my heartache and made many mistakes along the way. I did have a lot of fun, like a kid in a sweet shop, but it was bittersweet at times. I grew tired of the online addiction so I took six months off dating. I went on a solo yoga retreat, spent quality time with friends. Then I fell in love with a friend. For me, a real-life connection was nicer and more genuine than what I found online.

When I was single, I was very lonely at times. Self-love is essential but on a lonely Friday night, the need to be validated and held was overwhelming. Especially at the beginning.

It gets easier. It takes a lot of time and practice to heal. My tips? Time, more time and counselling, yoga, girlfriends, flirting and dancing and cocktails. You will get there, we all will.

Love,

Annie

HEARTWORK

Books to read:

Wild: A Journey from Lost to Found by **Cheryl Strayed**
Devastated by grief, Cheryl Strayed decided to hike more than a thousand miles of the Pacific Crest Trail from the Mojave Desert through California and Oregon to Washington State. It's funny, it's thought provoking, it's a distraction through tough times and it shows how you need thinking time to process your thoughts. Oh, and that far from being a negative, time alone can be truly enlightening.

Good Vibes, Good Life: How Self-Love Is the Key to Unlocking Your Greatness by **Vex King**
Vex King's Instagram messages will resonate with anyone going through a turbulent time. They make you feel hopeful and understood. His book achieves the same thing, using meditation, mindfulness and tried and tested techniques to overcome fear and help you feel good about yourself again.

CHAPTER ELEVEN

Sex
('Mum, you can do it once for your self-esteem')

'The best way to get over one man is to get under another'

Sex. Remember that? Has it been so long you feel like you've physically returned to a virginal state? And I'm guessing sex with your ex pre-split was hardly fucking joyous.

In the dying days of my marriage, I became the sexual instigator in a way I never had before. I was desperate for closeness. Desperate to re-establish our bond. X was reluctant. Perhaps because his desire was elsewhere. Or perhaps because it was over for him. Either way, it made me feel pathetic. It was debasing. Sex was laced with desperation, hurt, angst. It made me feel worthless. And I reflect now that maybe my disinclination to have sex over the years had done the same to him.

Because the truth is, we got together so young that the whole passionate, insatiable honeymoon period of sex never happened for me. Perhaps because our first sexual encounters were tempered with teenage angst. I was clueless. And frightened of making a fool of myself.

When the men I've dated since separation talk about sex with their previous long-term partners, they all bemoan the lack of passion, spontaneity and excitement. No fucking on the kitchen counter. No nights of multiple orgasms. No change to the old routine. It is always one of the reasons that they wanted to move on. They couldn't face staring down the barrel of ever-decreasing sex, or no sex. Couldn't face a life devoid of passion.

Though X and I had a lot of regular sex over the years and it was good, I was rarely the initiator, even pre-kids. (Is this TMI? Well, TMI is my MO, so buckle up.)

Did having children change your desire levels? It did mine. Suddenly my body was pulled and prodded all day. By babies that wanted feeding, by toddlers that wanted closeness. I stopped feeling sexual. I stopped feeling sexy. I think this was because I felt undervalued. Or just harassed. And rather than a hot, desirable career woman, I felt like the child carer, the lunch maker, the taxi driver. I saw myself that way and perhaps he saw me that way.

We lost what experts refer to as our 'sexual currency'. Keeping up your sexual currency is about positioning each other as desirable. Where you keep up the chemistry and maybe a bit of mystery, where you still flirt and tease and flatter. The opposite of going to the loo in front of each other or farting on the sofa, essentially.

In the post-baby years I was constantly, permanently, off-the-scale knackered. I had bags under my eyes that would surpass any airline's allowance. So I slowly shut down erogenous zones. Sealing them off, like aristocrats do with the rooms of a stately home they don't have the time or energy to keep open.

I always laughed with my friends that sex was like going to the gym. You had to make yourself but once done you felt much better. I know I wasn't alone in this, because my friend N told me that her idea of a good time in the bedroom was if her husband made it really quick so she could get to sleep sooner.

And I can see now how a future of this kind of 'oh go on then' perfunctory sex must have felt bleak for X. I didn't really consider my sexual future and I certainly didn't think of his. I was pretty proud we still had a regular, fulfilling sex life. Lots of my friends were doing it once a month at most.

How was sex in your relationship before your split? Maybe it wasn't earth-shattering movie sex. Maybe it wasn't hot and exciting every time. But it was safe, right? And your ex knew your scars. Mentally and physically.

Maybe post-childbirth sex is not the same for them either. Robbie Williams once compared watching his wife give birth to someone setting fire to his favourite pub. Which is pretty un-PC, but truthful at least.

OK, OK – so that was sex in your old life but, the chances are, unless you have sworn a vow of celibacy or are a devout Christian True Love Waits kind of person who is holding off till you are married again, sex with a new person is on the agenda now that you are single.

Contemplating exposing your body to someone new can be exciting. It can also be terrifying.

In order to look into the fears first, I met with Dr Karen Gurney. She's a psychologist, a self-styled sex doctor and the author of *Mind the Gap: the Truth about Desire and How to Futureproof Your Sex Life*. She told me, 'Body image is the number one sexual concern among women. While, interestingly, men's is performance.'

This rings true for me when I think of the conversations I have with my friends. Men are terrified at being found wanting in terms of virility while women are more anxious about their cellulite than whether they are going to have multiple orgasms.

Dr Gurney said, 'A lot of us women think that to be proud of our bodies, we have to conform to society's idea of what a sexy body is.' Basically, we feel like we need the body of a Victoria's Secret model in order to fulfil a partner. But we all know confidence is sexy. Sexier than flat abs and perky tits. If you believe you are hot, worthy, desirable, then so will your partner.

My male friends confirm this. And they swear it's not just because to say the opposite would involve them being roasted on the spit of political correctness. To add credence to this argument, a male friend pointed out that we don't go around insisting our lovers have a body like Jamie Dornan in the Calvin Klein ads, so why would it work the other way round? And it's true. In fact, the idea of some perfectly buffed specimen is fairly unappealing to me, to be honest. Give me a little wolfgang overhang and a few extra pounds over a gym obsessive with a puffed-out chest and chicken legs any day. My (male) friend B used to say, 'It's so weird to think a woman thinks I am scoring her body against an imaginary checklist when all I'm thinking is, woo hoo! I'm in bed with a naked woman.'

When I asked Dr Gurney about how women can get over their body image paranoia, she spoke about finding body positive role models. If porn is your thing, she suggests seeking out Erica Lust and her 'made by women for women' porn. It's female friendly and it holds up all body types as sexy. And shows that rounded curves can be just as desirable as washboard abs. In fact, probably way sexier to most men.

Talking of confidence, do you feel hamstrung by a lack of experience?

I do. I mean, the notches on my bedpost are embarrassingly low. For those of us who have been in a long-term relationship, the last time we were showing off our sexual skillz, Tony Blair was in Number 10. I fear that not being exposed to many different men, nor many different scenarios, means my sexual development kind of froze at my university self. And while I can see my university self was pretty pert (I wish I had appreciated this more at the time), she was also pretty naive. I've never seen porn (does *Porky's*, that 80s teen flick, count?) and never really deviated from the 'sexual shorthand' my ex and I devised in our teens. We established what worked for us and for years we were doing 'tweak here, push there, stand there' sex on autopilot.

If you are fairly unworldly, there's that paranoia that you are doing things wrong. Like that famous 'penis beaker' thread on the Mumsnet message boards, where one woman asked if it was normal to keep a glass of water on the bedside table for post-sex dick dunking. Er, no . . .

In short, are you, like me, worried you will be shit at sex?

To get intimate with someone is so exposing. It requires being vulnerable at a time when your self confidence is at an all time low. And yet . . .

I'm also feeling sexual excitement I haven't felt for decades. I had sidelined that side of me but now, in this new world of possibility, it's one of the true pluses. The kisses and the flirting with new men has ignited the pilot light of lust. Suddenly I can see the potential for pleasure and I'm ready to embark on a sexual odyssey. I know there will be frightening, exposing moments but I've learnt you need to grab life with both hands.

For the first time ever I feel unabashed sexual desire. Sexual desire not clouded by teenage angst, or shame, or fuelled by alcohol. I feel bad because it wasn't that X wasn't sexy enough or desirable enough, it's just I was sexually immature.

Part of this journey we are all on is the potential for a whole new world of sexual pleasure. Because, while our splits have swiped away the cosy future we envisaged, it's also offering us the chance to experience the thrill of kissing someone new, of sleeping with someone new. Fuck the slide into elasticated waistbands and madeira, this is about lacy underwear, about delicious anticipation. About butterflies in your stomach and morning sex and not being able to wait till you can get back home to rip each other's clothes off.

My friend, who split up with her husband eighteen months ago, told me, over a latte, that rediscovering the life-enhancing joy of sex was the best thing to have come out of a shitty time. 'It's fucking amazing. My husband hadn't touched me for years. We were basically like housemates. I felt so undesired. I felt dead between the legs. And now I can't get enough.'

She's not the only one . . .

SEX 2.0

Karen Gurney thinks sex in a new relationship is 'a massive opportunity. You can do something unusual for you but they don't know that. It's a freedom'.

I think if I'd have tried something experimental with X he'd have been more surprised than the nation would be if Prince Andrew revealed he had a first in astrophysics. On reflection, I think he'd have been delighted. I'm sorry to say I'd have shut him down.

How do you feel about sex with someone new? It can make us feel vulnerable of course, but do you feel it's tied up in the act of cementing a new relationship? And what is the etiquette these days? Wait till the fourth date? Or the tenth?

In *It's Just a Date*, authors Greg Behrendt and Amiira Ruotola–Behrendt say, 'We love sex and like to hear people are having it. We also think if you really like someone you should wait to have it. Not for some moral or chaste reason but because you have a much better chance of becoming a couple if you do.'

They argue sex changes things, and I know this is true for me. Some people can have sex without involving their emotions but I'm not one of them. Be honest with yourself about whether you're a free love kind of person or not. Greg and Amiira say that sex shouldn't be 'the carrot you dangle to get commitment' but instead something reserved for an exclusive, committed relationship.

This correlates to what guys I know tell me. That sex too early messes things up. The book says to wait ten dates or a minimum of three to four weeks of dating, which feels overly prescriptive to me. I think you have to trust yourself to know when the timing is right. (And I'd like to say that some friends of mine shagged the first night and are still together and happy, twenty-three years later, so there are exceptions.) But I do still think Greg and Amiira are onto something.

Ask yourself: do you want a committed relationship or just a shag?

Elizabeth Day told me that, after her marriage and a subsequent relationship, she went through a stage of 'having sex like a man'. She wasn't looking for commitment. Just pleasure. If this is you, then copulate whenever you want.

Do you want to enjoy sex but feel that something's stopping you? Perhaps for you sex has been about duty? Or fertility? Perhaps it is clouded with shame? Or in your relationship it became about power? Anyone emerging from a long-term relationship is likely to be carrying some sexual baggage. The good news is that you can reframe sex. Like you can reframe everything else.

I'm in my forties and in my formative teenage years the girls that enjoyed sex were called, variously, slags, slappers, whores, tarts, sluts. And the main preoccupation of mothers was to stop their daughters getting pregnant and 'throwing their lives away'. So sex was BAD. And that meant you treated it with a degree of distain, holding back on saying what you wanted, being passive, pushing down your desires.

'Traditionally there's so much shame around sex,' says Flo Perry, daughter of artist Grayson and psychotherapist Philippa, and author of *How to Have Feminist Sex*. Flo is terrifyingly millennial. She was born in the year I went to university, has dyed orange hair and is bisexual. She thinks we have been conditioned to push down our sexual wants because, 'It's been in the patriarchy's interest for women's desire not to be prioritised.'

I know this is true for me and the women I grew up with. We came of age in a time of *Loaded* magazine and *Maxim* covers, of 'get your tits out for the lads', where being thought of as sexy was the be-all-and-end-all. Note: 'being thought of as sexy'. Not feeling sexy. Our concern was all about how desired we were, not about any desire we might have felt ourselves – that was somehow secondary.

Dr Gurney agrees, adding, 'I write a lot about how women are socialised not to be assertive, to put others' needs above their own, and that also translates to sex. We are conditioned not to be overly sexual or sexually confident.'

Did women of my generation hand our sexual confidence over to our partners, instead of claiming it for ourselves?

One night when I have managed to pack the kids off to bed before I pass out through tiredness, I watch an episode of the Netflix docuseries *The Goop Lab*, focusing on the female orgasm. On the show, Goop's chief content officer, Elise Loehnen, says, 'We've been taught not only not to name our desires but to not

231

even acknowledge that we have them.'

When it comes to initiating sex, I think women of my generation can feel they make themselves look needy. Which is sad when, according to Dr Gurney, the statistics show that when women initiate sex they enjoy the encounter more.

Well NEWSFLASH. Sometime in the last few decades (when some of us were watching *Teletubbies* 24/7 and pureeing sodding carrots), unbeknownst to me, a quiet sexual revolution occurred. The shame around sex was dissolving. And . . . men, well, most of them, actively want you to enjoy it. My thirtysomething friends tell me that, at their schools, the cool girls were always having lots of sex. SO hello . . . This is your chance to learn, explore, experiment. Say what you want in bed, what turns you on, what feels great. What you don't want. This might feel cripplingly embarrassing, especially if you haven't been used to talking about sex with a partner. But it's important. If you seize this opportunity, this is the pot of gold at the end of the rainbow. You are free to have great, passionate sex.

Elizabeth Day told me that after her divorce, 'I thought how much am I missing out on? Sex had always been fraught for me. About "pleasing my man". It took till I was in my late thirties to get in tune with my own body.'

Sex is important. It's probably why you flipped to this chapter first . . . But why? Flo Perry says, 'We

socially bond through sex, it's a form of communication. Which is why you often have deep chats after it.'

And Karen Gurney agrees – she is passionate about
spreading the message that good sex is not just about
penetrative sex and orgasms but communication,
honesty and intimacy. When you put it like that, sex
becomes less about perfect bodies and bedpost notches
and gymnastics and more about something to look
forward to.

A word on sex with your ex

This is a well-trodden path. I hardly know a person who
hasn't been here (although I haven't) and I also hardly
know a person who hasn't regretted going here. Think,
really think about why you are doing it . . . preferably
before you have shared a bottle of wine. Are you trying
to show them how sexy and hot you are? What they
are missing out on? Is there are spark of hope for you,
or for them? Are either of you hoping sex will fan the
tiny flame into full blown fire?

IN WHICH CASE DON'T DO IT.

Are you lonely?

IN WHICH CASE REALLY DON'T.

I mean, there might be some world in which sex with
your ex is a good idea, but it's most likely a fantasy one
where houses are made of cheese. In reality, sleeping
with your ex keeps you in the relationship. It keeps

you emotionally stuck. If they are in your head, your thoughts, how can you move on? Avoid the headfuck that comes with the powerfully bonding chemicals released during sex. Save those for someone who deserves them.

Let's not beat around the bush

And in the spirit of moving on – can we talk pubic hair . . .

'Green,' says my mate N, 'no one under thirty-five expects to see hair down there.'

WTAF? Nothing . . . ??

So it seems like the grooming game has gone pro in the last ten years. The short back and sides bikini wax is as outdated as a flip-down Nokia. But I would say, from canvassing a vast sample on this matter (a lot of friends, male and female, not that many sub thirty-five), that it's personal choice. Whatever that choice turns out to be, here is some helpful grooming terminology:

Hollywood wax – everything gone – front, underneath, even round the arsehole. Expect to look like Barbie.

Brazilian wax – all hair from down below but leaves a landing strip at the front.

French wax – this is different in different salons but think removal of anything that would show outside of a skimpy pair of knickers.

The full bush – making a comeback. Sometimes more is more.

What you do is up to you. Have a bush, go bare. Just own it.

Underwear

Which brings me to the underwear drawer.

What does yours look like? I've got underwear older than Billie Eilish. Pants that have been in circulation since before Instagram was a thing. There are some thongs from the nineties (see, I told you . . .) but thank god they have been retired from duty.

(Sidenote: what happened to VPLs? We were all obsessed and thus started wearing thongs. Now we don't wear thongs and we don't have VPLs. What gives?)

Anyway, as part of my recovery, part of seeing myself as a wanton sex goddess (Bridget Jones's words) I decided to invest in underwear. I didn't have any money but I scoured the sales and the outlet sites. I manged to find matching sets that were pretty, not porny. Hot but not trash. And when I wear them, I feel great. Try it. It's impossible not to feel better when you are wearing gorgeous lingerie.

Worst thing to hear while having sex

A young man said to my friend mid intercourse, 'Make your pussy tighter.'

To which she replied, because she is fabulous, 'Make your dick bigger.'

Worst thing for your kids to hear is you talking about sex

Flirty chat is sexy, revealing, risqué, but what if your kids get wind of this whole new world opening up? It's a cringe for them to think of you as sexually active. (*If you are reading this, kids, then I'm sorry.*)

Suddenly your phone may be full of 'private' texts which your children might get a glimpse at as you are sitting on the sofa next to them. This often precipitates having 'the talk', but the other way around. When I told my tweenage daughter I was going on holiday with a boyfriend she asked me, in a completely matter-of-fact manner, if I was going to have sex while I was away. This was so shocking I nearly drove the car into a bollard. While I was still processing the question, she said that she thought my sleeping with someone would be a bad idea. As I tried to formulate an answer, she added coolly, 'Well, OK, Mum, you can do it *once* for your self-esteem.'

No words . . .

Dear Rosie,
I have been a fan of your brilliant Red *columns for years and I was saddened to read about the end of your marriage. Unfortunately, I experienced the same heartbreak several*

years ago; my ex-husband had a 'relationship' with a much younger work colleague and decided he didn't want to be part of our family any more.

There was a period of time when I had no idea what he was up to. I had put his regular and random outbursts of anger and horrific criticism down to work stress. I tried harder to be a better wife which actually just made him even crosser. Being a kind, thoughtful and understanding partner clearly just hindered his exit plan.

Of course, some of the harshest criticism was directed at our sex life, or lack of. We had been married for over twenty years having met at university and have three children. He travelled extensively with his job; weekends were spent ferrying the kids around activities and seeing friends and family. I had become, in his eyes, a boring, unattractive housewife and definitely wasn't sexy at all – he would tell me that he felt sorry for me.

Anyway, I could rattle on about that whole crazy time but I'd rather do a 'Rosie' and look for the silver lining.

He'd left, I was broken and lost, I could either sink or swim.

One day a good friend said to me, 'You're going to have to start being a little selfish if you are going to survive.' I started to take care of myself a bit better.

Time passed and another friend suggested I join a dating app. I was so apprehensive but after a couple of weeks I began chatting to a nice guy, we exchanged flirty messages on WhatsApp for a few weeks, then Facetimed. We agreed to meet for lunch. I was nervous but excited. My self-esteem was improving but still very low. I called my super stylish friend who told me exactly what to wear and my sister took me shopping. I changed my hair and got my nails done.

We met for a long, lovely lunch and more fun dates followed, it was exciting, I felt attractive/sexy again and he was kind to me. And he obviously fancied me. After a few months seeing each other, he suggested a spa day (gulp – that involved being semi-naked).

The day out somehow turned into a night away; he called to ask which treatments I would like and then asked, 'Should I book two rooms or one?' I didn't even take a breath and blurted out 'one'.

I went shopping for new underwear and a swimsuit, my friend told me to book a spray tan and my therapist told me just to have some fun!

The day arrived. We met at the hotel which was gorgeous, he'd bought me flowers and champagne and we spent a glorious day relaxing. Following a massage, we retired to our room . . . The sex was amazing. I had honestly subconsciously sidelined that side of my life. I didn't for a second think that I'd be having some kind of sexual renaissance.

I wanted to send you this letter, Rosie, because as horrific and broken as I felt post-split and still do at times, there are also exciting and lovely times ahead for us. This turned out to be a rebound relationship which helped me transition to the next chapter in my life. My married friends asked me if it was weird or uncomfortable sleeping with someone after only being with my ex-husband for twenty-plus years but,

to be honest, it felt more freeing than weird and more empowering than uncomfortable. I felt I was back!
    Love,
    Sam

HEARTWORK

Books to read:

How to Have Feminist Sex: A Fairly Graphic Guide by **Flo Perry**
Brilliant illustrations and acute observations make this book a compelling read. Talks about body shame and societal pressures and how open, honest communication is the foundation for good sex.

Mind the Gap: The Truth About Desire and How to Futureproof Your Sex Life by **Dr Karen Gurney**
Dr Gurney has counselled countless couples and this book shows how easy it is to lose your sexual spark, and also how it can be regained. It's full of revelatory facts (only 18 per cent of women orgasm during casual sex) and talks about how we are conditioned into thinking sex should be like movies (or porn).

CHAPTER TWELVE

Hope and Happiness
(rise like a fucking phoenix)

'Feel the sunshine on your face'

Now we are at the end, I remember the beginning. I remember googling in the early hours of the morning, unable to sleep, 'How long does it take to get over heartbreak?' Well, now I know the answers to some of those questions I was so desperately asking.

When will I stop waking up with that pit in my stomach? *Approx. five months*

When will I stop crying every day? *Approx. three months.*

When will I be able to contemplate a life without him? *Approx. six months*

When will I be able to contemplate a life with someone else? *Approx. six months.*

When will I be able to hear a Sam Smith song without feeling a stab of pain? *Approx. never. But this might be more to do with the scrotum-shrivelling high notes, than the poignancy of the lyrics.*

This is not what you want to hear at the beginning of the journey but time lessens the pain. Even in the time it's taken to read this book you feel a little better, right?

It takes time for your new reality to normalise. What is intensely painful in the beginning becomes less so. I used to feel so, so sad locking the door at night, with just the three of us inside. Now it actually feels cosy. I feel contentment as the bolt slides into the barrel. And now we all know that, while we slip back sometimes, and feel sad and anxious, we will feel better the next day.

I now know there is never such a thing as truly healed, because those scars will always remain, but so will the resilience and the self-knowledge.

What does being 'over it' look like to the outside world? To friends, family, Facebook friends and Instagram followers? Is it about finding love and skipping off into the sunset with a strong-jawed man who thinks you are amazing?

And fuck knows that makes life easier. I have found someone. I'm not going to lie. It feels good. Who knows what the future holds? But right now, in this moment, I am happy, and after what I've been through I don't take that for granted.

It would be untruthful to say that a new romance wasn't a large factor in my current contentment. I recognise that it buffers me from the vagaries of life, the tricky conversations with X, the anxieties about finances and the future. But one major lesson I have learnt from all this is: live in the now.

It might go wrong tomorrow. You might lose your home, your kids might meet your ex's girlfriend who might be the Amal Clooney lookalike, you might have to subsist on Kwik Save Baked Beans (does Kwik Save still exist?).

But what I wish I'd known then, is to just deal with what is happening right now. That's it. Trouble comes, trouble goes, but don't go looking for it. I've also learnt that real healing comes from rebuilding your self-esteem. From understanding that relationships fail but that doesn't mean you are a failure. This thing that happened in your life – it's shit, but it really is a gift. Because you don't want to be with someone who doesn't want to be with you. Or isn't right for you. You deserve more than that.

I have found it enlightening and empowering to realise that a lot of the pain of heartbreak is wrapped up with the fear of being alone. After a separation or a divorce, life might not be on the course you thought it would take but it will offer up experiences you would never have had were you still in your relationship.

'Sometimes the things that are best for you won't come in the package that you anticipated,' Elizabeth Day says. 'But you have to allow that to happen and give opportunities the space to flourish. There's no

242

point living your life according to your projected self. I used to be someone with a five-year plan. Now I feel so much more present and content when I'm just open to possibilities as they arise.'

Nothing is certain and there is a comfort in that if you learn to lean into it and accept it. The fear of uncertainty drives so many of us. For me, it meant I clung on tight to a relationship that wasn't good enough. Truth is, at my lowest point, I would have taken him back on any terms because the alternative was so terrifying.

Now we have faced those fears, you and I. We know we can survive on our own. There will have been countless shitty times but we are still standing. Heartbreak brings you to your knees but it's not fatal, and that's liberating. It teaches us that we don't need anyone to complete us or to rescue us. Healing comes from realising your own worth and building your resilience. Which is a far better strategy than going for a 'safe bet' partner.

Brené Brown, research professor and relationship sage, believes that resilience is the key to finding happiness in all areas of life. She says that, when it comes to team sports, the players everyone wants on their team are not those with exceptional skills and ability but those who know how to keep going, despite setbacks and difficulties. The player who gives it their all, every time, no matter how discouraging the odds, inspires others because 'that's what courage looks like'.

Pushing on, finding alternatives, refusing to give up. Haven't we done all that and more?

Can you reframe this shitstorm as a positive? Your life will be 100 per cent better if you do.

Once we understand the brain works in weird ways, that it triages information in a way that is not helpful, that our subconscious makes decisions that don't necessarily serve us best, we can resist our base reactions and instead search for the truth.

Does happiness lie in forgiveness?

'You can forgive him if you want,' my friend says. 'I'm not going to.'

What I struggle/struggled to forgive was what I felt was X minimising my pain, transferring his shame onto me by twisting his actions to make it my fault. And the ferocity of his anger and his lack of compassion for me. But now, as time has diluted the hurt, I can see he felt trapped and unhappy and didn't see a way out. And if he allowed himself to feel any of my pain, he would not be able to go through with leaving. So I choose to forgive. I want to forgive.

Studies show that letting hostility fester can lead to depression, anxiety, cardiovascular issues, immune system problems and higher risk of stroke. It's also exhausting.

Do you struggle with forgiveness though? I struggle with being nice, with being friendly to X because I feel that if I do I am condoning his behaviour. Showing him that it was OK to treat me that way. But at what

244

point do we move on, move past having to prove our point? I mean, friends can hurt us, family can do things that are 'wrong' but we forgive them. We let it go. We can see past it. We don't get caught up in it. We don't need to prove them wrong again and again. So why is it harder with our ex?

Well, because in a romantic relationship our ego is caught up in their behaviour. So when it comes to X, I try and see the situation from a mutual friend's point of view. As if you are looking at them through that lens. Not that of a disappointed partner. Your ex may have been a cheat/bully/delete as applicable. Or maybe he just wanted something or someone else. Does that make him a bad person forever?

Hopefully time will make, or has made, us realise they are fallible. And that means that we are fallible too. And if we can see that, if we can remove our ego from the situation, we can free ourselves from a world of anger and hurt.

You don't have to parcel up forgetting with forgiving but if you share children and you need to communicate with your ex, it makes YOUR life easier if you can be calm, considered and gracious. Just as long as you hold firm on your boundaries. If you have kids, you are likely to have to go to weddings, parties, graduations together. How much better for you, for them, for the kids, if it can be pleasant.

If you hold out the olive branch, your ex will most likely respond in kind.

Researchers and clinical psychologists Drs Julie and John Gottman, who have spent years working with couples on relationships, say that by taking responsibility for your part in the break up, you will shift the dynamic of your relationship. 'One person's response will literally change the brainwaves of the other person. Apologise to the other person when appropriate. This will validate their feelings and promote forgiveness and allow you both to move on.'

My friend Ruby Hammer, the make-up artist who has an abundance of inner and outer beauty, had a marriage which imploded in a similar fashion to mine two decades ago. With the perspective of twenty years' hindsight, she admits that forgiveness takes time. 'I said I forgave but I didn't really mean it. I wanted to be that person who forgave. I kind of faked it till I made it. Then one day, I was standing in the sea and I thought, "Fuck me, I really have forgiven him." I think it's about creating those new neural pathways, thinking it until you really mean it. Now we have an amicable relationship. We are never going to be best pals but we're good.'

While we are talking forgiveness, what about all those that couldn't or wouldn't help us when we really needed them? Not everyone can handle the shitstorm that you're in. And that's OK.

God, look how grown up and mature we are being.

I ask the beatific Ruby how she moved forward: 'With introspection, with learning lessons, with awareness, by

246

talking and rehashing and growing as a person.'

Addressing your role in the breakdown is like cleansing a wound with Dettol. It stings like fuck but recovery is quicker and the scars heal better.

I can see now that my ex and I are very different. We want different things. We love different things. Apart from our children. We both love them.

How is your relationship with your ex now? Have you managed to move into a place where you can recognise your differences without being tortured by them?

I can see so much of the conflict between X and me post-split was about miscommunication. And if every conversation and interaction is sullied with the desire to punish each other, it escalates tension. We didn't consciously uncouple like Gwyneth and Chris but I have started to recognise what I had at first fiercely rejected about their smug-seeming divorce statement, sifting out all the hurt and the anger from the way we deal with each other makes way for something new. Not necessarily perfect, but something less fraught and with more goodwill on both sides.

So, have I returned to the contentment of my old self? That innocent woman, undiminished by rejection, untainted by the dissolution of her safety and security.

No. The pain is always there. But so is a new strength.

Pippa Grange reminds me of the Greek philosopher Heraclitus's saying, 'No man ever steps in the same river twice, for it's not the same river and he's not

247

the same man.' She advises, 'The water has moved on. The opportunity is to think, "How do I grow and how do I get wiser?" We don't go back to who we are. We never revert to our former best. We become reshaped.'

I am reshaped. Rosie 2.0.

You are . . . [insert name] . . . 2.0

You may have a new partner. You may not. But what's important is self-love. And the knowledge you can survive anything. Neither of those things can ever be taken away without your permission.

Love yourself. Know your worth. And the rest will follow.

Here's the last letter. I wish I could have read this in those desperate few months when my heartbreak was fresh and raw.

Dear Rosie

I wanted to write to you to let you know you will be OK. In fact, you will be more than OK, you will be grateful for this painful, shocking, heart-wrenching experience. You will rise like a fucking phoenix.

I know every day you wake shaking with fear and damp with sweat, sucker-punched by your new reality but I promise this will pass. Because that old cliché is true, time heals.

I'm not going to sugar-coat it, it's profoundly sad that the children have had to deal with their cosy, secure lives being smashed into a million shards but actually isn't life at home calmer now, less fraught, with more love and kindness? And

248

you know what? They got to see that you survived and you were there for them. You can be so proud that you showed up for them, literally (fuck knows how you held it together in front of the kids the nights he didn't come home) and emotionally (the times you held them and listened to them when you felt you had nothing left).

You survived the loss of the only man you'd ever loved and the emotional roller coaster of divorce. Yes, there were shit times, lots of them actually, and sometimes you'll still hanker after your cosy secure life pre-split, where the bathroom tiles and curtains were your biggest worries.

I want to tell you if this hadn't happened you would not know how truly amazing your friends and family are. Nor would you have seen the depth of their love for you. That they would show up for you in a way that takes your breath away. You would not know that you had the strength to survive and actually thrive without the safety net of a partner. You will be liberated by this. Now you know you can do it alone if you have to. And how incredible that you found a way to turn this into an opportunity to help others, to tell their stories and bring shame and secrecy that has long surrounded separation and marriage failure out into the light.

Life would have continued on the path of domesticity but this way you got to feel, really feel again. Some of this was unutterably shit. The heart-cleaving sadness, the ego-crushing experience of rejection. But some of it was amazing. The thrill of the kisses with someone new.

And your career. You are literally front-page news. Your writing has its passion, its purpose back. I mean it made you write a book, FFS. Finally. Because it would take something this monumental to make you do that. Otherwise you would still be procrastinating and talking gardening schemes at the school gate.

There will still be bad days, I'm afraid, and you will be pumped full of adrenalin for a long time yet with a new challenge each day, but all the stuff you hate – the three signatures on the cards instead of four, the enforced time apart from the kids – will normalise to the point that it doesn't hurt any more.

You will surprise yourself with what you learn about yourself. Lots of this is positive but some self-reflection will show you where your negative behaviours have come from, when you are acting out of fear of abandonment or not being good enough. You will, in time, accept X's reasons and though you will not forget, you will forgive. You will be able to have friendly conversations with him and come together when the children need you to.

Though I would not for one second have wished this for you, it's given you a second shot, Rosie. A second shot at happiness, a second shot at a life that is built around your ideals, your wants and needs. A second shot of a relationship that's based on who you are now, not who you were at eighteen.

So, to summarise, you've smashed this shitball out of the park. I'm proud of you.

All my love,

Rosie

P.S. The best thing you ever did was get a dog. It loves you unconditionally, never says 'I'm confused', is always happy to see you and never farts in bed. ★

★*OK maybe the last one isn't true.*

HEARTWORK

Books to read:

Conversations on Love by Natasha Lunn
Tash is not only a brilliant and insightful and inspiring writer (and she really is) but a friend. She is the features editor at *Red* and almost a decade my junior. And while I was going through my split she was going through her own agony, trying to conceive and suffering a devastating miscarriage. In her book, *Conversations on Love*, she gets right to the heart of a subject that dominates our lives, taking us through the complexities of three questions: How do we find love? How do we sustain it? And how do we survive when we lose it?

RESOURCES

Nicky Clinch www.nickyclinch.com
Guy Winch www.guywinch.com
Malminder Gill www.hypnosis-in-london.com
Fiona Murden www.fionamurden.com
Sara Davison www.saradavison.com
Andrew Marshall www.andrewgmarshall.com
Pippa Grange @pippagrange (Instagram)
Sarah Lambert www.bowles-solicitors.co.uk
Relate www.relate.org.uk
Viva Mayr www.vivamayr.com
Nahid de Belgeonne www.thehumanmethod.co.uk
Fiona Lamb www.fionalamb.com
Collaborative Law www.resolution.org.uk/collabora-tive-practice/
Lisa Conway Hughes www.misslolly.com
Natasha Lunn www.conversationsonlove.co.uk
Dr Karen Gurney www.thehavelockclinic.com
Michelle Roques-O'Neil www.roquesoneil.com

Books to Read:

I Can Mend Your Broken Heart by Hugh Willbourn and Paul McKenna
How to Fix a Broken Heart by Guy Winch
Runaway Husbands: The Abandoned Wife's Guide to Recovery and Renewal by Vikki Stark
It's Called a Breakup Because It's Broken: The Smart Girl's Breakup Buddy by Greg Behrendt and Amiira Ruotola-Behrendt
The Unexpected Joy of Being Single by Catherine Gray
How to Fail: Everything I've Ever Learned from Things Going Wrong by Elizabeth Day
Heartburn by Nora Ephron
Leave a Cheater, Gain a Life: The Chump Lady's Survival Guide by Tracy Schorn
Tiny Beautiful Things: Advice on Love and Life from Someone Who's Been There by Cheryl Strayed
Poems for a World Gone to Sh★t by Various Poets
The Boy, The Mole, The Fox and The Horse by Charlie Mackesy
Rising Strong by Brené Brown
Everything I Know About Love by Dolly Alderton
Everything Is Figureoutable by Marie Forleo
Eat, Pray, Love: One Woman's Search for Everything by Elizabeth Gilbert
The Switch: The Secret to Overcoming the Pressures of Perfection and Finding Health and Happiness by Amanda Byram
Sex and the City by Candace Bushnell

254

It's Just a Date: How to Get 'em, Read 'em and Rock 'em by Greg Behrendt and Amiira Ruotola-Behrendt
Wild: A Journey from Lost to Found by Cheryl Strayed
Good Vibes, Good Life: How Self-Love Is the Key to Unlocking Your Greatness by Vex King
How to Have Feminist Sex: A Fairly Graphic Guide by Flo Perry
Mind the Gap: The Truth About Desire and How to Future-proof Your Sex Life by Dr Karen Gurney
Conversations on Love by Natasha Lunn

ACKNOWLEDGEMENTS

I would especially like to thank my dream team. My amazing publisher, Pippa Wright, who believed in me and this book and whose encouragement, empathy and editing made this process a joy. And not forgetting my brilliant agent, Becky Ritchie, whose enthusiasm and support gave me the space and security to tell my story.

Thank you to my amazing family and friends, without whom this book wouldn't exist. Without whom I wouldn't exist.

My deep, deep gratitude to all the people below, whose love and support gave me the strength to go from heartbreak to happy:

A
Robin Abeyesinhe

B
Nadine Baggott

Lady Baker
Caroline Barnes
Gemma Bateson
Sue Bird
Olivia Bloom Davies

Bee Bowman
Jodie Brinson
Kath Brown
Kelly Brown
Viv Brown
Helen Bruce
Charlotte Butterworth
Amanda Byram

C
Jo Cammel
Victoria Chalmers
Lorraine Clarke
Nicky Clinch
Lisa Conway Hughes

D
Jenny Davies
Nat Davies
Sara Davison
Elizabeth Day
Emma Dawson
Jess De Bene
Tania Devereux
Lindsay Derbishire

E
Miranda Elliott
Zoe Evans

Susannah Evans Pollard
Louize Evison

F
Sian Felwick
Liz Fergusson
Jamie Fergusson
Emma Fergusson
Colin Fergusson
Sarah Fergusson
Hilary Forrester
Shelia Forrester
Lindsey Frankel
Helena Fisher

G
Matthew Giles
Malminder Gill
Shoshana Gillis
Alison Green
Geoff Green
Saska Graville
Clare Griffin
Liam Griffin

H
Newby Hands
Ruby Hammer

Maxine Hanrahan
Ed Hanrahan
Sue Harmsworth
Harry Hopkinson

I
Claire Irvin

J
Nicola Jeal
Liz Jones
Annabel Jones

K
Camilla Kay
Kiki Koh

L
Amanda Lamb
Sarah Lambert
Tom Leman
Sophie Leman
Pete Leman
Nicki Leman
Richard Leman
Amy Le Roux
Matt Lever
Emily Lewis
Natasha Lunn

M
Sarah McKechnie
Fi Magill
Simon Magill
Shelley Marks
Andrew Marshall
Rachel Martin
Annabel Meggeson
Mihaela Melinte
Olivia Morris
Brigid Moss
Nicola Moulton
Fiona Murden
Mairead Murphy
Chris Murphy

N
Andrew Nesbitt

O
Marie O'Riordan

P
Kirsty Perkinson
Sue Pemberton
Lee Pycroft
Caroline Pierrepont

259

R
Ellie Radziwell
Anna Roberts
Sam Rogers
Tony Rogers
Nicola Rose
Amy Richardson
Jane Richardson
Sam Richardson
Chloe Reeves
Nick Reeves
Jacqui Ripley

S
Nikki Spoor
Ann Stewart
George Stewart
Will Stewart
Arthur Strong
Fifi Strong
Andy Swain
Leanne Swain

T
Ali Truesdale
Penny Taylor
Sarah Tomczak

V
Mat Venn

W
Jemima Walsh
Chris Walsh
Nikki Wellspring
Angela Wheatcroft
Nicki Wright
Richard Wilcox
Jules Woodall
Jo Vincent

Y
Lisa Youngs